In Defense
of Revolution

In Defense of Revolution

THE ELOHIST HISTORY

Robert B. Coote

FORTRESS PRESS   MINNEAPOLIS

IN DEFENSE OF REVOLUTION
The Elohist History

Cover illustration: detail of *Jacob's Dream* by Paul Gustave Doré

Cover and interior design by Jim Gerhard

Library of Congress Cataloging-in-Publication Data

Coote, Robert B., 1944–
    In defense of revolution : the Elohist history / Robert B. Coote.
        p.   cm.
    Includes bibliographical references and index.
    ISBN 0-8006-2496-3
    1. E document (Biblical criticism) 2. Bible. O.T.—
Historiography.   3. Jews—History—To 586 B.C.—Historiography.
    I. Title.
BS1181.2.C66   1991
222'.1066—dc20   91-19500
                                           CIP

Manufactured in the U.S.A.   AF 1-2496

95   94   93   92   91   1   2   3   4   5   6   7   8   9   10

As for the popular leader, . . . exiles, executions, hints of cancellation of debts and redistribution of land follow, till their instigator is fatally bound either to be destroyed by his enemies, or to change from man to wolf and make himself a tyrant.

Plato, *The Republic*

It is much safer to be feared than loved. Men loving according to their own will and fearing according to that of the prince, a wise prince should establish himself on that which is in his own control and not in that of others; he must endeavor only to avoid hatred.

Machiavelli, *The Prince*

Let them hate, so long as they fear.

Accius, in Suetonius, *Caligula*

Still thou art blest compared wi' me!
The present only toucheth thee:
But och! I backward cast my e'e
      On prospects drear!
An' forward though I canna see,
      I guess an' fear!

Burns, "To a Mouse"

Contents

Preface

This is an interpretation of E, one of the three basic strands of text in Genesis and Exodus. To understand the first books of the Bible, it is necessary to understand, among other things, E.

Of the three strands, E is the shortest, which partly explains why it has received the least attention. It is also true, however, that the classical literary analysis of the first four books of the Bible is currently somewhat outmoded, due to scruples and reservations old and new and, more particularly, to the growing realization that readers play a major role in determining the meanings of a text. The newly important reader has tended to place more emphasis on the apparent text and less emphasis on the more elusive historical writers and their text as the product of a process of writing.

This book takes a historical approach, with a view to addressing, by implication, the more important of the critical reservations regarding E. The historical approach continues to be the best way to discover clues to the meanings of a text that lie beyond ourselves as readers, to the extent that such discovery is possible. Moreover, I continue to agree with the principles of historical criticism—doubt, analogy, and the interconnectedness of everything—which together suggest that to understand a text, the reader must ask about things that are neither in the reader nor plainly in the text.

This book presupposes my work *The Bible's First History*, which deals with the J strand, the foundation for the E strand.[1] You might read the earlier book first, but that is not essential. What you need to know from it is sketched in chapter 7.

1. Robert B. Coote and David R. Ord, *The Bible's First History* (Philadelphia: Fortress, 1989).

I thank the many students in my classes on this subject going back for sixteen years, along with my colleague Marvin Chaney, Nathaniel Gray Professor of Hebrew Exegesis and Old Testament at San Francisco Theological Seminary and the Graduate Theological Union, for their sharp-eyed criticism, suggestions, and encouragement. I am likewise indebted to the late John A. Hollar of Fortress Press, whose memory continues to inspire, and to Marshall D. Johnson, editorial director of Fortress, and his staff, whose perspective, aid, and support prove repeatedly vital. My constant partner in writing remains my wife Polly.

Introduction

The first four books of the Bible, or the Tetrateuch, form one continuous text. The division of the Tetrateuch into four books came late in its development and was quite incidental, having to do largely with how many lines could be written on a single manageable scroll. Although the Tetrateuch is continuous, it was not all written at the same time under the same circumstances. Instead, it was produced during nearly five hundred years of writing and rewriting. It makes sense, therefore, to view the Tetrateuch in terms of a process of writing with discrete stages rather than as four separate books. To understand the Tetrateuch, it is necessary to understand how as a whole it came to be written in stages.

J, E, AND P

The Tetrateuch consists of three kinds of text, or strands, called J, E, and P. These strands differ, but their purposes are the same. They represent three overlapping legitimating histories of cult that were composed for three successive rulers or ruling groups at the start of their rule, when each seized rule from another: J in the court of David, E in the court of Jeroboam I, and P in the court of the Jerusalem temple priests of the early Persian period. This book is about the second kind of text, or strand, E. Small additions were also made under Hezekiah, after the writing of E and before the writing of P; these will be considered briefly in chapter 13.[1]

1. For a concise introduction to the writing of the Tetrateuch and the rest of the Bible, see Robert B. Coote and Mary P. Coote, *Power, Politics, and the Making of the Bible: An Introduction* (Minneapolis: Fortress, 1990). For the nature and importance of royal ideology, see Keith W. Whitelam, "Israelite Kingship: The Royal Ideology and Its Opponents," in *The World of Ancient Israel: Sociological, Anthropological and Political Perspectives*, ed. Ronald E. Clements (Cambridge: Cambridge University Press, 1989), 119–39.

The Tetrateuch began with J, which was written early in the tenth century B.C.E. in the court of the warlord David, who captured Judah and Israel from the house of Saul. From J the Tetrateuch acquired its basic narrative outline. J was a history of the world and of "Israel" (Judah and Israel) designed to reflect the rise of the house of David and to buttress David's rule against the threat of Egyptian invasion.[2]

Over the next five centuries, two major overlapping supplements were made to J—E and P—along with at least one significant minor one, to produce the Tetrateuch in its present form. The Tetrateuch is thus the result of a series of overlapping supplementations of J.

The first major supplement was E, the subject of this book. E was written in the court of Jeroboam I, king of Israel. Jeroboam rose to power in the revolution that at Solomon's death overthrew the house of David in Israel. (The house of David held on to Judah.) Jeroboam ruled Israel for twenty-two years and passed his kingdom on to his son. As a usurper, Jeroboam took pains to assert the legitimacy of his rule and the jurisdiction of his law, especially in opposition to Solomon's son Rehoboam, heir to the much-shrunken realm of the house of David. As expected, court literature played a role in Jeroboam's quest for legitimacy. As ruler of Israel, Jeroboam appropriated J, David's history of Israel. However, he did not leave J as it was. He instructed his scribe, or agreed to his scribe's initiative, to recopy it and incorporate supplementary narratives and laws. These supplements were added to nearly all parts of the original except, untypically, its beginning and end. These supplements are E. The combination of original J and supplement E, David's history of Israel and Jeroboam's additions, are JE. In my view, which will be explained in more detail shortly, E never existed except as a part of this combination. The text of E does not, and never did, tell a connected story without its J framework.

JE reflected the new ruler's claim to legality and continuity. Its most attentive audience was Jeroboam himself. Jeroboam also had it read to the strongmen of his realm to encourage their loyalty. Furthermore, he targeted it back over the border to Rehoboam and his retainers, hoisting the house of David with its own petard. In light of J, Solomon's rule had been no better than pharaoh's. JE gave Jeroboam the right to supplant the house of David. As far as is known, Rehoboam took no notice. He kept J the way it was, with only minor changes in which he maligned Jeroboam's state cult at Bethel.

The view of this book that E reflects Jeroboam's experience of the revolution is based on circumstantial evidence. It is a new attempt to

---

2. Robert B. Coote and David Robert Ord, *The Bible's First History* (Philadelphia: Fortress, 1989).

make the best possible sense of the evidence regarding E. Others will have to judge how likely this view of E's origin appears in comparison with alternative, equally circumstantial views. This book's positive tone should not mislead newcomers to the discussion into thinking that matters are as settled as this book may on occasion inadvertently make them sound.

The minor supplement to the Tetrateuch was the work of a writer back in the house of David, in Jerusalem in the late eighth century B.C.E., during the reign of Hezekiah. This writer added to JE several paragraphs whose style looks back to J and forward to the Deuteronomistic writings. This supplement was designed to help the house of David repossess their history of Israel as amended by the addition of E. The Israelite state had fallen in 722 B.C.E., leaving JE without an official repository. Under Assyrian domination, Hezekiah, recalling the house of David's claim to sovereignty over Israel, endeavored to attract northern strongmen, proponents of JE, to his vassal sovereignty. The anti-Egyptian thrust of JE also matched Assyrian policy. The enlarged corpus of laws in this newly supplemented JE enhanced the ability of the house of David to exercise jurisdiction again beyond the bounds of Judah.

The other major supplement was P, the priestly strand of the Tetrateuch. P latched on to the cultic subject of JE and recast the venerable history into a literary vehicle for the essential rites and laws of the dominant expatriate, then resident, class of Jerusalem priests at the beginning of the Persian period. These priests were the heirs of Davidic rule following the Babylonian exile of the house of David and its failure to recover under Persian rule. Loosely speaking, the priestly supplements include many of the additions in Numbers that may have been inserted or affixed after the main composition of P. This priestly tradition goes back to the monarchic period, but in its present written form it constitutes the latest strand of the Tetrateuch.[3]

Of these three supplements, E added the bulk of new narrative, making J about a third longer. However, unlike J, E is found only in Genesis and Exodus. In addition, E added new laws to J's small corpus of laws, along with adding many extensions and short isolated phrases to J stories. The purpose of this book is to explain how the narratives, laws, and supplementary phrases of E modify J to reflect the anti-Davidic revolution in Israel under Jeroboam. As explained in this book, E was propaganda in defense of revolution in late tenth-century B.C.E. highland Israel. Jeroboam also defended the revolution with

3. Robert B. Coote and David Robert Ord, *In the Beginning: Creation and the Priestly History* (Minneapolis: Fortress, 1991).

strength of arms, the reconsolidation of state jurisdiction, the restruc-
turing of the cults of Israel, and a royal building program. His literary
propaganda was just one of several means to strengthen his rule.

In one sense, E as understood here is almost unique. In the nautilus
that is the Bible, nearly every chamber favors the house of David or
their priestly successors in Jerusalem, in rivalry with the heads of
other regions and centers (not the least the Palestinian northern highland). E stems from, and favors, the rulers of the northern heartland of
Israel and their factions; it is one of only two or three parts of the Bible
to do so. Others include parts of the narratives about Elijah and Elisha
and a handful of individual psalms.[4] None of these match in either
length or substance E's contribution to the perennial struggle of northern rivals and rebels against Jerusalem. In JE is found, for example, the
self-presentation of the same Jeroboam whose abomination was a pillar
of Jerusalem-based Deuteronomistic propaganda. JE promotes the revival of the monarchy of the same Saul defamed by Jerusalem publi-
cists from David's time on. It is the one book in the Bible's library to
tell the story for the kings of Israel and against the house of David
without hedging.

Its story is David's story, however, in more ways than one. In JE's
defense of Israel's revolution lies disguised the rise of Jeroboam, a
replica of the rise of David. Both rulers co-opted resistance movements
propelled by people in distress, and each then employed scribes to
justify his takeover as the local liberator—the self-aggrandizing, alien-
backed highland warlord who as king assumed sovereignty over the
grain lands of the villagers under his rule. David and Jeroboam had
much in common. Between the end of the eleventh century and the end
of the tenth, circumstances had changed, most notably through the
entrenchment of state rule under the Davidids. Nevertheless, David
and Jeroboam were of a type, in relation not just to each other but to
numerous other tough, lucky usurpers in the history of Palestine.

The privileged justifiably fear the usurpation of rule. Jeroboam
was no exception. The fear of God that figures so largely in E includes
fear of a usurper. Like the privileged in all times and places, Jeroboam
fears himself in other men, and he feels compelled to project this fear,
in the form of judicial respect, or "the fear of God," as public policy.
The security of the state, embodied by Jeroboam and elevated in the
disposition of the awesome and hope-filled fear of God, failed to safeguard his people's welfare. Jeroboam saw violence only in others and

---

4. Gary A. Rendsburg, *Linguistic Evidence for the Northern Origin of Selected Psalms*
(Atlanta: Scholars Press, 1991).

hence could not have foreseen the judgment of God in the fall of Samaria and Jerusalem, nor have imagined that the state and its god, rather than controlling violence, are the origin of violence.[5] In this deception, Jeroboam was merely one with the "ruling orders" of all ages, whose "need to see themselves consolingly reflected in a world of their own creation" gave us E—and J and P.[6]

This book begins in chapter 1 with a description of what E is, how it is discerned, and how best to make sense of it. Chapters 2, 3, and 4 present E in three nearly equal parts, with enough of J included to show clearly how E all along relates to J. Chapter 5 examines Solomon's tyranny; chapter 6, Jeroboam's revolution; and chapter 7, how Jeroboam read JE back at Solomon's son Rehoboam.

The division of E into three parts is not only an editorial convenience but also an intrinsic feature of the text. The main division comes with the disclosure of God's cultic name Yahweh and its meaning at the site of the sanctuary Horeb (Exod 3:9–15). Everything following this division has to do with Horeb, the model for the jurisdiction of Jeroboam's state cult. The narrative before this division also deals with cults of Jeroboam's kingdom, but its distinctive subject is sons in mortal danger. Joseph, who stands for Jeroboam and Israel, is the prime example of a jeopardized son and so receives special attention as the subject of a separate section. Thus, the text has three divisions: sons, the son Joseph, and Horeb.

These three parts of E form the subject of chapters 8 through 12. Chapter 8 treats E's stories of sons in danger; chapter 9, the expanded story of one such son, Joseph, who represents the heartland of the revolution and the "tribe" of Jeroboam; and chapters 10, 11, and 12, the country shrines of E, their rituals and practices, and their jurisdictions and laws.

The conjunction of E's main concerns defines Jeroboam's engrossing anxiety for proprietary legitimacy and dynastic inheritance. What right does Jeroboam have to own the rule of Israel? Can he pass his rule to his son? These are the two basic questions that preoccupied the royal patron of E and find their reflection in E's stories and pronouncements. The former question is implied often in the Old Testament. It may not at first coincide with what we expect the Bible to be about. However, the surprise is no greater than when a student of Shakespeare, for example, first realizes that Shakespeare wrote in support

5. Pierre Clastres, *Society against the State: Essays in Political Anthropology* (New York: Zone Books, 1988).
6. Terry Eagleton, "The Ideology of the Aesthetic," *Times* (London) *Literary Supplement*, 22–28 January 1988, 94.

of Tudor legitimacy in *Richard III* near the beginning of his career (to
assuage the anxiety of the heir of Henry VII, who may himself have
had the princes in the Tower killed) and, as writer for the King's Men,
in support of Stuart legitimacy in *Macbeth* shortly after the accession
of James VI of Scotland over England as well.[7] The second question,
regarding succession, is also implied often in the Old Testament,
though possibly less often than the first.

Chapter 13 deals with the eighth-century proto-Deuteronomistic
repossession of JE by Hezekiah mentioned above, through supplements to JE that have sometimes not been distinguished from E. Chapter 14 reflects briefly on the implications of the view of E presented
here.

The analysis of the Tetrateuch into its constituent strands, known
now for a century and a half, has mattered little, even to the few aware
of it. As for the present, readers of all kinds of persuasions increasingly
prefer to believe that books of the Bible form wholes more than parts,
that the Bible belongs more to its living readers (whose concerns impose
themselves regardless) than to its dead writers, and that the Bible
makes more sense in terms of what is familiar than what is not. What
does it mean, after all, to "make sense," if not to admit and take advantage of the reader's intrusion in the process? This intuition of more
convenient access to the Bible, based on premises in themselves largely
valid, is served by superior works of scholarship, whose number grows.[8]

7. Beyond such straightforward correspondences lie the many more subtle, pervasive, and
basic ways in which literature reflects political forces and circumstances, an awareness of
which is essential for understanding literature: for Shakespeare, see the brilliant treatment
by Leonard Tennenhouse, *Power on Display: The Politics of Shakespeare's Genres* (New York:
Methuen, 1986).
8. For Genesis and Exodus, recent studies include J. P. Fokkelmann, "Genesis" and
"Exodus," in *The Literary Guide to the Bible*, ed. Robert Alter and Frank Kermode (Cambridge: Harvard University Press, 1987), 36–65; Thomas W. Mann, *The Book of the Torah:
The Narrative Integrity of the Pentateuch* (Atlanta: John Knox, 1988); Suzanne Boorer, "The
Importance of a Diachronic Approach: The Case of Genesis-Kings," *Catholic Biblical Quar-
terly* 51 (1989): 195–208; Frank Crüsemann, "Der Pentateuch als Tora: Prolegomena zur
Interpretation seiner Endgestalt," *Evangelische Theologie* 49 (1989): 250–67; Walter
Brueggemann, "Genesis," in *The Books of the Bible*, ed. Bernhard W. Anderson, vol. 1 (New
York: Scribner, 1989), 21–45; Nahum M. Sarna, "Exodus," in *The Books of the Bible*, ed.
Bernhard W. Anderson, vol. 1 (New York: Scribner, 1989), 47–62; David J. A. Clines, *What
Does Eve Do to Help? and Other Readerly Questions to the Old Testament* (Sheffield:
Sheffield Academic Press, 1990), 9–105. For an assessment of the most recent computer
research on the matter, see G. J. Wenham, "Genesis: An Authorship Study and Current
Pentateuchal Criticism," *Journal for the Study of the Old Testament* 42 (1988): 3–18;
Stephen Portnoy and David L. Peterson, "Statistical Differences Among Documentary
Sources: Comments on 'Genesis: An Authorship Study,'" *Journal for the Study of the Old
Testament* 50 (1991): 3–14. For the modern development of reader-centered interpreta-
tion, see the comments of Sean E. McEvenue, "The Elohist at Work," *Zeitschrift für die
alttestamentliche Wissenschaft* 96 (1984): 315 n. 1, and the excellent introduction by Edgar
V. McKnight, *Post-Modern Use of the Bible: The Emergence of Reader-Oriented Criticism*
(Nashville: Abingdon, 1988). For a stimulating attempt to treat the text of Genesis on the
basis of the classical strands, see Bruce Vawter, *On Genesis: A New Reading* (Garden City,

It lies quite within the scope of adroit interpretation to ignore the distinctiveness of E and to blend E with J and P, as the final text and all translations do in any case, in order to enhance the text's accessibility.

On closer examination, however, much in the Bible is found to be not conveniently accessible. The E strand, although not easily discernible to the reader of the English Bible even after close study, nevertheless does form a distinctive part of Genesis and Exodus whose existence must be accounted for and respected, and the observant reader will find this strand, once discerned, not altogether amiable. So much is indisputable. E's assumptions and expectations, its concerns and emphases, its style and form are not what most readers are used to or necessarily expect. To make sense of E, and not to ignore it, requires us to acknowledge its author's foreignness while at the same time approaching his writing confident that what he has to say, as much as we can discover it and understand it, will be worth the inconvenience of finding it out. (We're not sure of the identity of the author of E, but it seems likely that the person was a man, so we use the pronoun he.)

The dead may thank us for thus respecting them, though that is not sufficient excuse for this book or any other written from a historical perspective. The diversity of human apperception in ages past is like the diversity of life in the present. The extinction of the least of ancient apperceptions constitutes a grievous and fateful loss and portends the disregard of its counterpart in our time, as well as of the history of the construction of meanings essential to understanding our own history. Until E makes sense on its own terms as well as ours, it is an endangered species of apperception, to say nothing of biblical faith. Although the task must remain incomplete because our knowledge of the history of the Bible and its world is incomplete, nonetheless it lies with us, as readers of the Bible and as human beings, to bring E back from near extinction.[9]

N.Y.: Doubleday, 1977). For an assessment of recent trends in literary criticism from a perspective alert to historical criticism, see Terry Eagleton, *Literary Theory: An Introduction* (Oxford: Basil Blackwell, 1983).

9. This book proposes what to many is bound to seem a surprisingly particular and definite origin of E, and in this regard as well may appear to oppose the trend, even in interpretation that is still primarily historical, to develop the generic more than the specific context of a writing. Generic and comparative considerations play a large role in what follows, as will be seen. However, since an important part of what is generic about the context of E is political usurpation and the scriptural construction of a royal office, there is little reason to avoid deciding *whose* usurpation and *which* royal office are most likely involved, when circumstantial evidence points heavily in the direction of a specific instance, namely Jeroboam I and the kingship of Israel. This time, settling for generalities would be arguably more naive than venturing specifics.

CHAPTER ONE

What Is E?

E is a group of texts in Genesis and Exodus with a set of characteristics distinguishing it from J and P. E also refers to the supposed author of this group of texts. Before the middle of the nineteenth century, most historians thought Genesis and Exodus were composed of only two kinds of texts, one using the name Yahweh for God and the other, simply God. The first they called J (for *Yahweh*) and the second E (for *'elohim*, Hebrew for God).[1] In 1798 K. D. Ilgen and in 1807 W. M. L. de Wette observed that in a number of places the second kind of text actually contained a third kind. Little came of this observation until in 1853 H. Hupfeld restated it in persuasive detail.[2] Hupfeld convinced many historians that the second group of texts, the "God" texts, consisted of two different groups. The first began in Genesis 1, dealt with priestly matters, and was much the larger of the two. The second began in Genesis 20 (some scholars detected a verse or two in earlier chapters) and, once pointed out, looked quite unlike the first. Historians eventually named the first "God" group P, for its priestly character. The second kept the designation E. Since then the study of the three basic kinds of text has been much refined, but the basic three remain the same: J, P, and E.[3]

---

1. The J comes from the European use of *J* for *Y*. Many English translations avoid *Yahweh*. Substitutes include LORD, GOD, and *Jehovah*. Readers of the English Bible should accustom themselves to noticing that *Yahweh* occurs in the text underlying these substitutes.
2. H. Hupfeld, *Die Quellen der Genesis und die Art ihrer Zusammensetzung* (Berlin: Wiegand & Grieben, 1853). See Paul Volz and Wilhelm Rudolph, *Der Elohist als Erzähler: Ein Irrweg der Pentateuchkritik?* (Giessen: Töpelmann, 1933), 2–3; Karl Jaroš, *Die Stellung des Elohisten zur kanaanäischen Religion* (Göttingen: Vandenhoeck & Ruprecht, 1974), 18–19.
3. For the history of scholarship, see Volz and Rudolph, *Der Elohist als Erzähler*, 2–11; Alan W. Jenks, *The Elohist and North Israelite Traditions* (Missoula, Mont.: Scholars Press, 1977), 1–18; Douglas A. Knight, in *The Hebrew Bible and Its Modern Interpreters*, ed. D. A. Knight and G. M. Tucker (Philadelphia: Fortress, 1985), 279–83.

CHARACTERISTICS OF E

E is recognizable where its distinctive vocabulary, style, preference of subjects, and point of view cluster in a given text. E uses *'elohim* for God, *Jacob* for Israel in the history of Joseph, *Horeb* for Sinai, *Jethro* for Moses' father-in-law, and *'ama* for a female slave. E's style is more earnest than J's: E presents life as a serious matter, involving critical turns of events. J's incessant punning is totally absent from E.

E's distinctive point of view and interests are the subject of this book and so can only be previewed here. E takes particular interest in the tribes of Israel who became part of the northern kingdom of Israel in the early monarchic period. E contributes nothing to the history of Judah. E takes interest in numerous sanctuaries but never Jerusalem nor any other shrine in Judah, with the possible exception of the tomb of Rachel, Joseph's mother. In contrast to J's frequent references to fieldstone altars, E makes much of the practice of setting up a menhir, or ritual upright stone, on which olive oil is to be poured. In contrast to J, in which Yahweh typically appears as a man standing next to a person in broad daylight, in E God appears at a sovereign remove, usually in a dream at night. In contrast to J's companionable Yahweh, E's God arouses dread. In E this fearsome God nevertheless commits himself repeatedly to "be with" the protagonist. E tells stories of sons at risk of losing freedom or life. In contrast to J, however, E shows God in complete control of events. Unlike J, E details the ins and outs of characters' responses and the subtleties of ambiguous legal situations.

These characteristics distinguish E from J and P, particularly where several characteristics occur together in the same text, as they usually do. Because P is quite distinctive, and because E is adjacent to, or entangled with, J much more often than with P, in practice the discernment of E amounts to distinguishing E from J.

E'S RELATION TO J

The definition of E is not quite so straightforward as this catalog of features might suggest. Disagreements about which texts belong to E, however, are likely to be based less on the identification of such typical features of E than on differing views of what E was, how it came into being, and how it was related to J. It is widely held that J and E are two different versions of one common tradition. In the light of this view, which I believe is erroneous, texts have been examined for minute signs of duplication on the assumption that two versions of a common narrative, similar to each other, have been combined in the existing text. A text that otherwise shows none of E's distinguishing features can thus be analyzed into J and E components on the basis of this kind of supposed duplication.

Moreover, if J and E were variants of each other, it would be reasonable to expect that at least some residue of E should be found to match all of J, from Abram to the end. This is not the case,[4] but the expectation is difficult to dispel. E does not in fact seem to occur in Numbers at all. However, since in E the name Yahweh is introduced near the beginning of the history of Moses—after less than two-thirds of J and much less than half the Tetrateuch—many historians have been tempted to assume that following the introduction of Yahweh, a text in which Yahweh appears may come from E, even though other features of E are missing and E clearly continues to use *'elohim* as well. Other texts are mistakenly assigned to E due to a failure to note that J itself uses *'elohim* at its beginning and end. The supposed E texts in the story of Balaam in Numbers 22–23 offer a prime example.

Such misconceptions can be clarified by a different notion of how E originated. It is useful to begin by distinguishing three types of E texts, although once the nature of E becomes clear this distinction becomes less important. The first type is the *whole narrative*. The first story from E, concerning Abram in Gerar, is an example (Gen 20:1–17).[5] Others include Abram's near sacrifice of Isaac (Gen 22:1–13), Joseph's interpretation of the cupbearer's and baker's dreams (Gen 40:1–23), and pharaoh's daughter's rescue of the infant Moses from the rushes (Exod 2:1–10).

The second type of text is the E text ostensibly *intertwined with J*. In intertwined texts, J and E seem to follow on each other with little rhyme or reason and are sometimes found to be difficult to disentangle. The first such text in E, and an excellent example, occurs when Jacob stops at Bethel in his flight from Esau (Gen 28:10–22). J explains that just as Jacob lay down to sleep, Yahweh appeared standing next to him to repeat the blessing he swore to Jacob's grandfather Abram, granting to Abram's descendants all the land visible from the height where Jacob was lying. Jacob exclaimed that the place must be Beth-El, the "House of God," and the portal to the sky. J says nothing about Jacob's ever getting to sleep, let alone waking up the next morning. Intertwined with this story are lines and phrases from E, which

---

4. The text of E is imbedded in the middle five-sevenths of J, in an irregular pattern attributable to E's purpose. The beginning and end of J are left unsupplemented. The reason for this distribution will become clear.
5. I assume that the form *Abram* occurred in both J and E throughout, and that when the change to *Abraham* was introduced into the continuous text by P (Genesis 17), the name *Abram* in later chapters was modified to make it consistent with this change. This assumption is not certain, however, since neither P nor later editors are regularly so consistent.

appear to depend on the framework provided by J. In the additions
from E, Jacob takes a stone for his pillow. He falls asleep without
interference and has a dream. In his dream he sees God at the top of a
palatial stairway busy with court messengers dashing up and down.
To Yahweh's pronouncement in J, God in E adds, "I am with you and
will watch over you and not abandon you until I have done all I have
told you." Then, in E, Jacob awakes in dread; remarks on how dread
the place is; sets his pillow stone upright as a menhir; pours olive
oil upon it; and vows that if God will indeed be with him, he will
solemnly return a tenth of his production to God at this shrine.

The third type of E text is the *isolated line, phrase, or word* embedded in a J narrative that otherwise shows no sign of E. For example,
when Jacob, on his way back to Canaan, meets up with Esau, E inserts
this brief exchange: "Esau said, 'Who are these belonging to you?'
And Jacob said, 'The children with which God favored your servant'"
(Gen 33:5; note the term God and E's special concern for sons). Jacob
repeats his point a few lines later, in a brief E fragment: "for God has
favored me" (Gen 33:11). When in J the Egyptian lord's wife tried
to seduce Joseph, he complained, "How shall I do this great evil?" to
which E adds, "and break the law against God" (Gen 39:9). Although
E nearly always left J intact, in a few places an E phrase may replace an
original J phrase. For example, E provides etymologies for the sons of
Jacob representing the northern kingdom that in some cases may replace original J etymologies. For Joseph, both J and E etymologies are
preserved (see Gen 30:1–24).

As the text of E in the next three chapters shows, these types of E
text are not sharply different. The story of Joseph's brothers' jealousy
toward Joseph and their selling him as a slave intertwines J and E texts.
Within this story, however, Joseph's dreams about ruling over his family (Gen 37:5–11) form nearly a whole E narrative, as comparison
with the dream narratives involving Joseph in Egypt indicates. What
is important is that E can appear in J in all three forms. An explanation
of E must account for this variety.

DIFFERENT FOUNDATIONS

Because E is shorter than J and P, it has received less attention. It has
been thoroughly studied, however. Most agree that E originated in
northern Israel in the monarchic period, between the accession of
Jeroboam I (931 B.C.E.) and the fall of Samaria (722 B.C.E.). There is no
reason to question this starting point. There is much less agreement
about who wrote it, why, and exactly when. Most interpreters regard
E as a quasi-prophetic document that criticizes the evil excesses of the

state. The object of this criticism might have been Jeroboam in the tenth century, the Omrid kings in the ninth, the elite condemned by Amos and Hosea in the eighth, or some other. Nearly every period in the two-hundred-year history of the northern kingdom of Israel has been suggested by one historian or another as the context of E.

These proposals tend to be based on somewhat improbable premises. As mentioned, it is generally thought that J and E were separate and complete variants of a common tradition. In this view, J and E both told the same story, with slight variations. One way to explain their similarity is to suppose that once one had come into existence in one of the two Israelite "nations," the other was produced in imitation of it in the second nation, as a repository for supposedly common traditions but in a version suited to the particular biases of the second nation. A variation on this explanation supposes that the common story existed first in oral tradition. Thus, E recorded stories that originally took shape as they were passed on by the "Hebrew folk." J and E were then supposedly (re)merged by an editor well after the writing of E. Where J and E said essentially the same thing, this editor gave precedence to J. In the present text, therefore, only "fragments" of E are preserved. Finally, it is assumed that since E consists almost entirely of narrative, in the discussion of E the portion of the law of Moses from E (Exod 21:1–22:16) can be ignored.[6]

I believe such premises are mistaken. The preferred alternatives are mostly not new but rather neglected in favor of those just explained. E probably originated as a written supplement to J and never existed apart from it. E was a product of the court. In passages where E seems to duplicate J, the scribe was using J as a narrative resource. E is not fragmentary in the sense that most of it is missing but in the sense that as a supplement to J, it was never meant to duplicate the whole of J but rather to use J as its basis. E is all there. The laws of E are integral to E and essential for understanding it. The following paragraphs look briefly at each of these premises.

E is a supplement to J and never existed apart from it. There never was an E without J. It would be more accurate to refer to E as (J)E, JE, or JE. (The last style, with E in boldface, is used to present JE in the following three chapters.) It makes sense to speak of the E strand but not of the E document. E assumes J throughout. E is not a variant of J or of some tradition common to them, so there is no point to using apparent duplication alone for distinguishing E from J. Many historians have

---

6. These ideas are widely held and appear in most critical commentaries and handbooks and in the most recent literature, even a work as inventive as Richard Elliott Friedman's *Who Wrote the Bible?* (New York: Summit Books, 1987), 83–85.

already understood E to be a supplement to J.[7] However, most of them understood E as a collection of random, incidental supplements made over many years, not a single coherent supplement made at one time. The view that E once existed independent of J is still widely held and taught, especially in the United States, largely because of the continuing influence of two important German scholars, Martin Noth and Hans Walter Wolff, and now of Alan W. Jenks in the United States.[8] Nevertheless, like most of the composite writings in the Bible, JE was in fact composed by supplementation rather than by the editing of two similar documents.[9]

When trying to make sense of E, it can be presumed that E refers to J. For example, when Abimelek says to God, "Would you murder a righteous people as well?" he is referring to Yahweh's destruction of Sodom and Gomorrah in J. E assumes Hagar and Ishmael returned to Abram, since in J, Yahweh instructed Hagar to return and submit to her mistress. When God calls Abram a "prophet," he is referring to Abram's negotiation with Yahweh over Sodom's fate in J. Such narrative allusions by themselves would not indicate E knew J in written form rather than their common ancestor in oral form. Noth proposed that E originally included the same stories as J but that the editor who combined J and E included only E passages that differed markedly

---

7. See, for example, Rudolph Smend, *Die Erzählung des Hexateuch auf ihre Quellen untersucht* (Berlin: Georg Reimer, 1912); Volz and Rudolph, *Der Elohist als Erzähler*; R. N. Whybray, "The Joseph Story and Pentateuchal Criticism," *Vetus Testamentum* 18 (1968): 522–28; Th. H. C. Vriezen, *An Outline of Old Testament Theology*, 2d ed. (Newton, Mass.: Charles T. Branford, 1970), 58; Sigmund Mowinckel, *Erwägungen zur Pentateuchquellenfrage* (Oslo: Universitetsforlaget, 1964), 59–118 (Mowinckel expressed this view as early as 1930); Hannalis Schulte, *Die Entstehung der Geschichtsschreibung im alten Israel* (Berlin: DeGruyter, 1972). These authors exemplify the diversity of opinion toward supposedly E material. Whybray, for example, has doubts whether the classical analysis of the Tetrateuch is correct at all.
8. Martin Noth, *A History of Pentateuchal Traditions*, trans. Bernhard W. Anderson (Englewood Cliffs, N.J.: Prentice-Hall, 1972 [German orig. 1948]), esp. pp. 20–41; Hans Walter Wolff, "The Elohistic Fragments in the Pentateuch," in *The Vitality of Old Testament Traditions*, ed. Walter Brueggemann and Hans Walter Wolff (Atlanta: John Knox, 1975), 67–82 (German orig. 1969; also *Interpretation* 26 [1972], 158–73); Jenks, *Elohist and North Israelite Traditions*. On this point, Noth's discussion was something of a response to the work of Volz and Rudolph, which after World War II was little heard of, especially as U.S. scholars came into their own in biblical studies. The current situation in the United States is not unlike what Volz described for Germany at the beginning of the century in *Der Elohist als Erzähler*, 3, 11–12: the currently prevailing view of the relation of J and E, for those concerned, borders on received dogma.
9. As early as 1906, E. Meyer emphasized E's "complete dependence" on J: *Die Israeliten und ihre Nachbarstämme* (Halle: Max Niemeyer, 1906), 17, 58, 74, 259, 276 n. 1, 323 n. 3 (cited by Volz and Rudolph, *Der Elohist als Erzähler*, 11 n. 1). Among recent interpreters, McEvenue appears to represent this view: "Elohist at Work," 329–30. Frederick V. Winnett, in "Re-examining the Foundations," *Journal of Biblical Literature* 84 (1965): 1–19, argued that E was an *official* revision of J. Although Winnett's views of J and the dates of the revisions differ from the ones held here, his notion of the growth of the Tetrateuch through authorized additions is essentially the same.

from J. However, J was court literature, not common Israelite national tradition. Moreover, the particular character of E sets it off altogether from J. Most important, the supposed editor of JE might have extracted the first type of E text, as Noth suggested, and possibly the second type, but this idea could hardly apply to the third type of E text, the isolated phrase.

In addition, there are places where E makes use of J phrases but gives them a distinctive E meaning. For example, in J, Yahweh appeared to Jacob at Bethel by "standing next to him," a common expression in J. E incorporates these same words from J but changes their meaning: Jacob sees a palatial stairway with God "standing on top of it."[10] Again, in J, during the time when Moses' people were enslaved, Moses "became important." E incorporates this same phrase from J to say instead that after the midwives saved the boy babies and pharaoh's daughter rescued Moses, Moses "grew up," consistent with the meaning of the phrase in E in Gen 21:8, 20.[11] Such literary use of J makes it likely that E came into existence attached to J.

Understanding E in relation to J therefore involves not so much figuring out how E differs from its supposed equivalent in J but rather explaining where in J a supplement or insertion is being made by E; what in J is being commented on, supplemented, or expanded; and in what way and why. Because every E text exists because of the E writer himself and not a later editor, all E texts, including isolated phrases, should figure, if possible, in the interpretation of E. Moreover, although it is important to understand the E texts in relation to one another, as Wolff brilliantly illustrated in his essay on E, it makes little sense to examine E texts by themselves, apart from their present relation to J.

E was a product of the court. Apparent duplications result from the writer's imitating J or reproducing J in his own version. Because E is a supplement to J, a concept of E requires a concept of J. Questions about the early history of traditions supposedly recorded in J and E have tended to dominate the investigation of E. These include the quest for Noth's "G" (for *Grundlage*, or "common basis") and Frank Moore Cross's "epic."[12] Incidents in E that duplicate J, like the first E story, concerning Abram in Gerar, do not go back to a supposed common tradition but are based directly on J, as many have previously

10. See Robert B. Coote and David Robert Ord, *The Bible's First History* (Philadelphia: Fortress, 1989), 153.
11. Coote and Ord, *The Bible's First History*, 11–12, 218.
12. Frank Moore Cross, *Canaanite Myth and Hebrew Epic: Essays in the History of the Religion of Israel* (Cambridge: Harvard University Press, 1973), s.vv. "Elohist," "Epic Sources."

proposed. This first E story combines elements from J's stories of Abram in Egypt and Isaac in Gerar. E was written by a scribe who studied the scroll of J, planned the insertions carefully, and then rewrote the scroll with the additions planned. E's supplements made J's narrative about one-third longer.

E is all there. It does not consist of "fragments" gleaned capriciously from a putative complete document to complement J where E departs most from the line they have in common, as suggested by Noth and Wolff. Noth used the notion that part of the original E was missing in E as it presently exists to suggest that originally E represented a supposed earlier stage in the history of tradition. As already mentioned, E is distributed more or less evenly over the middle five-sevenths of J.

The laws of E are integral to E and essential for its understanding, although most explanations of E omit them altogether. These laws occur at E's climax, in Exod 21:1–22:16. They are the focal point of E in the so-called exodus, JE's narrative tsunami. J, E, D (Deuteronomistic History), and P all combine narrative and law, and in all of them the combination is fundamental.

WHEN, WHERE, WHO, AND WHY?

Now that *what* the term E refers to has been discussed, it is time to introduce the other classical literary questions: when, where, who, and why? These go together. The full answer is the subject of the rest of this book. This section will note only the general framework within which most historians have placed E.

E is different from J, so its when, where, who, and why are probably also different from J's. If J comes from the south, or Judah, E probably comes from the north, or Israel (some speak of Ephraim to take advantage of its initial E). Most think E dates to the monarchic period in Israel, between Jeroboam I—its first king, whose reign began in 931 B.C.E.—and its fall with the Assyrian capture of Samaria in 722 B.C.E. The range of views as to exactly when E was written covers this entire two-hundred-year period. Probably the commonest view is that E is a quasi-prophetic narrative related to the antimonarchic stories of Elijah and Elisha in the ninth century or the great antielite prophets Amos and Hosea of the eighth century. The sole book-length treatment of E in English departs from this common view by placing E at the beginning of the period, in the reign of Jeroboam.[13] When Jeroboam established his state cult, he apparently degraded the traditional priests called the Levites: it is therefore reasonable to imagine

13. Jenks, *Elohist and North Israelite Traditions.*

that the antimonarchic quality of E might stem from a Levite author. The most recent U.S. treatment of E places this Levite in Shiloh, although not as early as Jeroboam.[14] These two studies advance the subject. Their main weakness is their dependence on problematic texts from Exodus (especially Exodus 32) and Numbers that probably should not be classed as E texts at all. The classical literary questions do continue to hinge on the identification of E texts. It thus seems preferable to base the interpretation of E primarily on the most generally agreed upon E texts of Genesis and Exodus.

Norman K. Gottwald understands E as being "apparently intended as a conscious corrective to the J document." While suggesting the likelihood that E was written during the ninth century, perhaps in reaction to the ruling house of Omri in Israel, he observes, as many have, that E appears to have an "antique" quality that suggests a premonarchic origin. Gottwald says, "In E there simply is not the same focus on land and state that there is in J." Because these supposed early E traditions predated the Israelite monarchy and appeared to find fault with the monarchy, "it is not likely that E was written in court circles," as is often suggested for "its southern counterpart J."[15] Gottwald's concise statement correctly appraises E's stance toward J, even though it shares the prevailing assumption that J and E were versions of the same original tradition.

E stands, then, for *'elohim,* its preferred designation for God; Ephraim, its place of origin; enhancement, its textual relation to J; and earnestness, its critical stance toward J and the monarchy. And for elite, as it was likely written in the court of the king of Israel and in this regard was similar to J. These and further traits will be presented in more detail in the following chapters, which develop the view that E is critical not of monarchy in general but of the house of David in particular, and of the house of David's pretensions as expressed by their own reading of J. By adding E, Jeroboam turned J into a version of the by then established court history of Israel that was friendly toward him and his own court.

THE CONTENTS OF E

As mentioned in the Introduction, E divides into three parts.[16] The first part tells stories about dangers to sons. Such stories continue in the second and third parts, which concentrate on two further

14. Richard Elliott Friedman, *Who Wrote the Bible?* (New York: Summit Books, 1987), 70–88.
15. Norman K. Gottwald, *The Hebrew Bible: A Socio-Literary Introduction* (Philadelphia: Fortress, 1985), 138, 350, 351.
16. See the list of E texts at the end of this book.

concerns of Jeroboam, the history of Joseph (the putative father of the heartland Israelites of Ephraim and Manasseh) and the cult of Horeb (the model of Jeroboam's state cult) and its laws. Dangers to sons, Joseph, and Horeb and its laws—these are the three subjects that stand out in the three main parts of E.

E enters J's history at the end of Abram's story, with the birth of Isaac. The paternity of Abram's son is jeopardized when Abimelek seizes Saray. Abimelek corrects his wrong just in time after God warns him in a dream. Ishmael is on the brink of dying when his mother runs out of water in the desert. Abram contracts with Abimelek for Beersheba. God tests Abram by ordering him, in a dream, to slaughter Isaac as an offering and then preventing him just in the nick of time. E next intervenes to enlarge on Jacob's founding of the cult of Bethel, which was essential to Jeroboam's state, after a dream in which God speaks to him. Children are born to Bilhah in place of Rachel, Joseph's mother, and then Joseph himself is born to Rachel. When Jacob, with his sons, are threatened by Laban with impoverishment, God rescues him. Jacob flees, but Laban overtakes him. In dire jeopardy, Jacob protests his innocence, and he and Laban, representing Israel and Aram, make peace in a ceremony elaborated on in E. Returning to Palestine, Jacob founds the cults of Mahanaim and Shechem, and of Deborah near Bethel, and confirms the cult of Bethel, all in Israel, while twice professing that it was by God's grace that his sons survived. Joseph's full brother, Benjamin, is born with Rachel's dying breath.

The narrative has reached the story of E's favorite ancestor. E declines J's change of Jacob's name to Israel, since Israel under Jeroboam excluded Judah and hence was no longer his "father." Joseph has two dreams that prove he was destined to lord over his brothers. When his brothers threaten to murder Joseph, it is Reuben, rather than J's Judah, who saves him just in time. For his determination not to break the law against God, Joseph ends up in pharaoh's prison, again at risk for his life. There he interprets dreams with God's help and comes to pharaoh's attention. By interpreting the dreams of pharaoh himself and advising him on how to obtain control of all the food in Egypt, Joseph gains his favor and is elevated to the position vizier of Egypt. The story of Joseph's ability to explain dreams is the longest in E. Joseph fathers Manasseh and Ephraim, the "tribes" of the heartland of Israel. When Joseph's brothers come to Egypt for food and he sends them back for Benjamin, he forces them to leave Simeon behind in jeopardy. When the brothers are reunited, Joseph professes that it was God who made him ruler over Egypt in order to save Jacob's sons from imminent starvation: "It was for saving lives that God sent me ahead of you." E expands on Jacob's frailty to introduce his blessing of the two sons of Joseph. E adds a special blessing of Joseph. Once Jacob dies, his sons begin to worry again that Joseph will take revenge. One word from him, and they are done for. Joseph reassures them in their jeopardy and forgives them: "You devised evil against me, but God devised that the same should be good, to achieve what he has today, saving the lives of a great people." Before Joseph dies, he enjoins his brothers to guarantee that his bones will be taken out of Egypt.

E's third section begins by elaborating on the birth of Moses, the founder of the cult of Horeb, with two stories illustrating the critical dangers this vital son of Israel faced at his birth. First, pharaoh orders all sons of Israel murdered. They are saved in the nick of time by the Israelite midwives. Then Moses is sent drifting in a box on the Nile and is "drawn out of the water" by pharaoh's daughter, again just in time. The rest of E concentrates almost entirely on the cult and laws of Horeb established by Moses. This climactic concern is marked with the revelation of God's name Yahweh to Moses at Horeb. There Moses fears to look at God. He is told, however, a sign that God is commissioning him to deliver his people: "When you have brought the people out of Egypt, you all shall serve God at this mountain." On that occasion, the very end of E, "they saw God." Moses leaves his father-in-law, Jethro, to see whether his people are "still living." When Moses and the Israelites flee Egypt, they make sure to take Joseph's bones with them. Moses appears back at Horeb with Israel, and Jethro comes to meet him. Jethro advises Moses on the hierarchical magistracy that is to characterize Israelite jurisdiction under Jeroboam. God flashes, thunders, and smokes from Horeb, threatening to kill the people. Moses reassures them in their jeopardy: "Fear not. God has come to test you (as he first tested Abram), so that the fear of God will be before you so you will not sin." Moses by himself approaches God and receives from God the law of the realm, detailed by E. Once the laws have been recited, Moses and his cohort feast with God; and Moses, the chief of Israel, again approaches God, alone.

Here, with the revelation of law at Horeb through Moses and the activation of its cult, the E additions to J end. Israel's wasteland trek, the rebuff of the challenges to Moses' authority, and the grand finale on the theme of blessing in the story of Balaam—these Jeroboam's scribe left as they are in J.

Certain recurrent themes distinctive of E are already evident from this epitome. Two stand out as particularly noteworthy: the dangers sons fall into and their rescue, and the shrines and cults of Israel, with their practice of incubation (seeing and hearing God in a dream). Everything in E, in one way or another, comes into contact with these two themes. E also frequently refers to cultic menhirs (upright stones), the fear (or awe or dread) of God, the assurance or wish that "God is with you," the characterization of Israelites as "alive" or "living," and the response "right here" to a summons. All these and more figure in the interpretation of E once the history of the revolution that led to its writing becomes clear.[17]

In the following three chapters, J appears quoted, paraphrased, or summarized, as appropriate, in regular type. E appears in full in bold type.[18] In this way, E's relation to J will always be clear.

17. For further reading on E not otherwise cited in this work, see John F. Craghan, "The Elohist in Recent Literature," *Biblical Theology Bulletin* 7 (1977): 23–35; Terence E. Fretheim, "Elohist," in *Interpreter's Dictionary of the Bible*, supp. vol., ed. Keith Crim (Nashville: Abingdon, 1976), 259–63.
18. The translation is by the author.

CHAPTER TWO

Sons

Yahweh created humanity. They behaved so badly that Yahweh placed several curses upon them. Eventually he blessed a man named Abram, who then behaved better. The blessing included the promise of a son, who, however, was a long time in coming. Saray, living with Abram at Hebron, eventually became pregnant with Isaac. **Abram pulled out from there toward the land to the south, and settled between Qadesh and Shur and so resided in Gerar. Concerning his wife, Saray, Abram said, "She is my sister."**

When Abimelek, the king of Gerar, sent men to take Saray, God went to Abimelek in a dream at night and said to him, "You are as good as dead due to the woman you took, since she is owned by an owner."

Since Abimelek hadn't gone near her, he said, "Would you murder a righteous people as well? Didn't he say to me, 'She is my sister,' and didn't she herself say, 'He is my brother'? I did this without any idea, and with guiltless hands."

God said to him in the dream, "I knew you did this without any idea, so I held you back from breaking the law against me. That's why I didn't let you touch her. Now return the man's wife. He's a holy man, so he may intercede on your behalf and keep you alive. If you don't return her, know that you and all yours will be dead."

First thing next morning, Abimelek summoned all his court followers and described all these things to them. The men were very afraid. Abimelek summoned Abram and said to him, "What have you done to us? In what way have I broken the law against you such that you should bring upon me and my kingdom a great violation? You have done with me deeds that are simply not done." Abimelek went on to Abram, "What did you see that made you do such a thing?"

Abram said, "I thought, 'There need only be no fear of God in this place, and they will murder me on account of my wife.' Anyway, she is my sister—my half sister, daughter of my father but not my mother. She became my wife. When God made me wander from my father's household, I said to her, 'Do me this favor in whatever place we get to: say about me that I am your brother.'"

Abimelek took sheep, goats, cattle, and male and female[1] slaves and gave them to Abram. Then he returned Saray, his wife, to him. Abimelek said, "My land lies before you. Settle wherever it pleases you." To Saray he said, "I just gave a thousand pieces of silver to your 'brother.' He is reason to keep your eyes covered near all who are with you, and especially those in front of you."

Abram interceded with God, and God healed Abimelek and his wife and servants, and they bore sons.

Isaac was born. Saray said, "God has made it for me an occasion for laughter. Everyone who hears will laugh at me."

When the boy had grown bigger and was weaned, Abram threw a big feast, on the day of Isaac's weaning. When Saray saw the son whom Hagar the Egyptian had born to Abram making like Isaac, she said to Abram, "Drive this slave away, and her son with her, so this slave's son will not inherit along with my son, Isaac."

This seemed an atrocious idea to Abram, since Ishmael was his son as much as Isaac. But God said to Abram, "Don't be overly concerned about the lad and your slave. Follow all the instructions Saray gave you, for your long line of descendants shall be through Isaac. However, I shall also make the slave's son into a people, since he is your offspring."

First thing in the morning, Abram took bread and a skin of water and gave them to Hagar. He placed these and the boy on her shoulder, and sent her on her way. She hiked off and eventually got lost in the desert of Beersheba. When the water in the skin had given out, she discarded the boy beneath one of the desert shrubs and went and sat across from it about the distance of an arrow shot, saying, "Don't let me see the boy's death."

As she sat across from it, she cried out and wept. God heard the lad's voice, and the genie of God called out to Hagar from the sky, "What's wrong, Hagar? Don't be afraid. God has heard the boy's

---

1. Hebrew *šipḥa* usually indicates J rather than E. It has replaced *'ama* because of this line's similarity with Gen 12:16.

voice and knows the boy is there. Go pick up the lad and hold his hand tight. I am going to make him into a great people."

Then God opened her eyes, and she saw a well. She went and filled the skin with water and gave the lad a drink.

He grew up and settled in the desert and became an archer. He settled in the desert of Paran, and his mother got him a wife from Egypt.

At that same time, Abimelek and Pikol, his commander, said to Abram, "Since God is with you in everything you do, swear to me here by God that you will not deal falsely with me and my progeny and posterity. I have shown you favor; show me and the land you are residing in the same."

Abram said, "I shall take this oath."

Later, when Abram was in dispute with Abimelek concerning a well Abimelek's men had seized, Abimelek claimed, "I don't know who did this thing. You hadn't told me about it, and I hadn't heard about it until today." So Abram took sheep, goats, and cattle and gave them to Abimelek, and the two made an agreement. Abram set seven ewe lambs apart. Abimelek said to Abram, "What are these seven ewe lambs you've set apart here?" Abram said, "You shall receive seven ewe lambs from me so that you will acknowledge on my behalf that I dug this well." That's why that place is called Beersheba [Swear-Well], since the two of them swore there. When they had made their agreement at Beersheba, Abimelek and Pikol, his commander, picked up and returned to Philistine territory.

After these events, God tested Abram as follows. He said to him, "Abram," and Abram said, "Right here." God said, "Take your one son, whom you love, Isaac, and go to the Land of Awe. There sacrifice him as a whole burnt offering, on one of the hills, the one I designate to you."

First thing in the morning, Abram saddled his ass. He took his two aides with him, and Isaac, his son. After splitting up wood for the offering, he set off for the place God would designate to him. On the third day, Abram raised his eyes and saw the place from far off. Abram said to his aides, "Stay here with the ass, while I and the lad go on a bit and worship, then return to you."

Abram took the wood for the offering and set it on his son Isaac, then took in his hand the fire and the knife. As the two strode together, Isaac said to Abram, his father, "Father," and Abram said, "Right here, my son."

Isaac said, "We've got the fire and the wood, but where is the sheep for the sacrifice?"

Abram said, "God will see to it for himself that there is a sheep for the sacrifice, Son."

As the two went on together, they came to the place God designated to him. There Abram built the altar and arranged the wood on it. Then he tied up his son Isaac and placed him on the altar on top of the wood. Just as Abram put out his hand and grabbed the knife to slaughter his son, the genie of God[2] called out to him from the sky and said, "Abram! Abram!" and he said, "Right here." And he said, "Don't strike at your son, and don't do anything to him, for now I know that you are so in awe of God that you did not hold back your one son from me."

Abram raised his eyes and saw a ram caught that very moment in the bush by its horns.[3] Abram went over and took the ram and burnt it as a whole offering in place of his son.

Isaac had two sons, Jacob and Esau. They competed against each other so that finally Jacob had to flee for his life. He traveled toward Aram and on his way came to the place that later became the Israelite sanctuary Bethel. When he arrived there, the sun was setting, and he decided to spend the night. He took one of the stones of the place and set it as his headrest. As he lay at that place, he had a dream in which there was a stairway with its base on the earth and its top reaching to the sky. There were genies of God proceeding up and down it, and there was Yahweh stationed at the top of it. He said, "The land you are lying on I will give to you and your descendants. You will spread out from here to the north, south, east, and west. I am with you. I will watch over you everywhere you go and bring you back to this land. I will not abandon you until I have done all I have told you."

Jacob awoke from his sleep and was afraid. "How awesome this place is. This is none other than the house of God, and the gate to the sky."

In the morning, Jacob took the stone he had set as his headrest, set it up as a menhir, and poured oil on top of it. Then he made a vow: "If God will be with me and watch over me on this journey I am making, and gives me food to eat and clothing to wear, and I return safely to my father's house, then this stone which I have set up as a menhir will be the house of God, and of everything you give to me I shall solemnly return a tenth to you."

---

2. Hebrew *yahweh* results from the influence of the non-E section in Gen 22:14–19. The E original had *'elohim*. Note the partial parallel in Gen 20:18, where for *yahweh* in the Masoretic text the Samaritan and some Greek manuscripts indicate *'elohim*.

3. See M. Pope, "The Timing of the Snagging of the Ram, Genesis 22:13," *Biblical Archaeologist* 49 (1986): 114–17.

Jacob came to Aram and married Leah and Rachel. Leah bore him four sons. When Rachel saw that she had borne Jacob no sons, she was jealous of her sister and said to Jacob, "Give me sons. If you don't, I might as well be dead." Jacob got angry with Rachel and said, "Can I take the place of God, who has held back from you the fruit of the womb?" She answered, "What about my slave Bilhah? Have intercourse with her, and let her bear 'on my knees,' so that I, too, can build my family, through her." So she gave Jacob Bilhah, and she bore Jacob a son. Rachel said, "God has judged me and also heard my voice and given me a son." Therefore she named him Dan. Bilhah bore a second son. Rachel said, "Wrestling like God I have wrestled with my sister, and prevailed." So she named him Naphtali.

When God listened to Leah, she got pregnant and bore Jacob a fifth son. Leah said, "God has given me my wage." So she named him Issachar. Leah bore a sixth son. Leah said, "God has given me a fine gift." So she named him Zebulun.

God remembered Rachel, and God listened to her and opened her womb. She got pregnant and bore a son and said, "God has gathered up my shame," and named him Joseph.

Laban and his sons began to resent Jacob, so Yahweh told Jacob, "Go home, and I will be with you." Jacob sent for his wives and flocks and said to them, "I have noticed your father doesn't look at me the same old way. But the God of my father is with me. You know that I have worked for your father with all my strength, yet your father cheated me and changed my pay ten times. But God did not let him do me harm. If your father said, 'I'll pay you the spotted ones,' the whole flock would bear spotted ones. If he said, 'I'll pay you the streaked ones,' the whole flock would bear streaked ones. In this way God delivered your father's livestock and gave them to me.

"In the breeding season, I looked up and saw in a dream streaked, spotted, and dotted he-goats mating with the flock. The genie of God said to me in the dream, 'Jacob,' and I said, 'Right here.' He said, 'Look up and see, all the he-goats mating with the flock are streaked, spotted, and dotted, for I have seen everything Laban has been doing to you. I am the God at Bethel, where you anointed the menhir, to whom you made a vow there. Now get right out of this land, and go back to your birthplace.'"

Rachel and Leah answered him, "We have lost our land and inheritance rights in our father's estate. We are regarded as foreigners as far as he is concerned, since he has sold us and squandered the money paid for us. Since all the wealth God has delivered from our father belongs to us and our sons, do everything God said to you."

Laban was off shearing sheep, so Rachel was able to steal her father's teraphim. Jacob fooled Laban the Aramaean by not telling him he was about to flee. Laban found out and caught up with Jacob at Gilead. God came to Laban the Aramaean in a dream at night and said to him, "Watch out you don't press Jacob about anything for good or bad." Laban asked Jacob why he had run off without a word and stolen from him. "If you had told me, I would have thrown a party. But you have acted foolishly. I have the power to do you grave harm, but your fathers' God said to me yesterday, 'Watch out you don't press Jacob about anything for good or bad.' Why did you steal my gods?"

Jacob said, "Anyone you find your gods with will not live. If in the presence of our kin you recognize anything in my possession that is yours, take it." Jacob didn't know Rachel had stolen them.

Laban entered Jacob's tent, Leah's tent, and the tent of their two slaves and did not find anything. When he had left Leah's tent, he went into Rachel's tent. Now Rachel had taken the teraphim and placed them in the camel's saddle basket and sat over them. When Laban had rummaged her entire tent and not found anything, she said to her father, "I hope my lord is not angry because I am not able to rise respectfully before you. I'm having my period." Thus, Laban searched everywhere but failed to find the teraphim.

Jacob got upset and said, "What did I do wrong, that you should rummage all my belongings? Did you find anything that belongs to you? Put it here in front of my kin and your kin, and let them decide between us. For the twenty years I've been with you, your ewes and she-goats have never miscarried. I have never eaten rams from your flock. I have never brought to you a torn-up animal, but have covered the loss myself. You have held me responsible for anything stolen, whether by day or night. I was . . . by day the heat consumed me, by night the frost, when sleep fled my eyes. I put up with this for the twenty years I worked for you in your household, and you changed my pay ten times. If the God of my father, the Fearsome One of Isaac, had not been by me, you would have sent me off with nothing. But God has seen my oppression and the hard work of my hands, and yesterday passed judgment."

Laban said, "Let's make a covenant." So Jacob took a stone and erected it as a menhir. So Jacob had his kin collect stones into a heap. There Laban and Jacob had a meal together and made their covenant. Laban said, "May Yahweh watch between us when we are out of each other's sight, to see that you don't mistreat my daughters. You see, God is a witness between you and me. This heap and the menhir

here which I have set up between us, this heap is a witness **and the menhir is a witness** that I not pass this heap into your territory and that you not pass this heap **and this menhir** into mine. May the God of Abram and Nahor judge between us"—**the God of their father.** **Jacob swore by the Fearsome One of his father Isaac.** Jacob and his kin then feasted there in the hill country.

In the morning, Laban kissed his daughters, bade them farewell, and returned home. Jacob continued his journey. **The genies of God bumped into him. When he saw them, Jacob said, "This is the camp of God." So he named that place Mahanaim [Two Camps].** Jacob sent messengers ahead to Esau, telling them to tell Esau, "I have become rich. I am sending this news to my lord to find favor with you." The messengers returned and told Jacob that Esau was already on the way with four hundred men. Jacob became extremely frightened. He divided his people and livestock into two camps. When Jacob crossed the Jabbok at Penuel, he wrestled with God's genie. As Esau approached his brother, first one camp and then the other went by, with Jacob at the very end of the line. When he finally got to Jacob, he looked and saw the women and children **and said, "Who are these belonging to you?"**

And Jacob said, "The boys with which God favored your servant."

When the slaves and their children and Rachel and Joseph had approached and bowed, Esau said, "Who were this whole camp of yours I just encountered?"

Jacob said, "It was for finding favor in the eyes of my lord."

Esau said, "I already have a great deal. Keep what you have."

Jacob said, "No. If I have found favor in your eyes, take my gift from my hand, for you have received me kindly. So take my blessing brought to you, **for God has favored me,** for I have everything."

The brothers parted, and Jacob continued his journey south. He arrived at Shechem and camped just outside the city. **He purchased the portion of the open field where he was encamped from the sons of Hamor, Shechem's father, for one hundred qesitahs. There he set up a menhir and called it El-is-the-God-of-Israel.**

An incident led to war with Shechem, and Jacob's sons captured and plundered the city.

God said to Jacob, "Get up and go up to Bethel and dwell there. Make there a menhir for the El who appeared to you when you fled from Esau, your brother."

Jacob said to his family and to all who were with him, "Put aside the gods of the foreigner in your midst. Purify yourselves and put on fresh clothes, and let us get up and go up to Bethel, so that I can

make there a menhir to the El who answered me on the day of my distress and was with me on the journey I took."

So they gave to Jacob all the gods of the foreigner that they had, along with their earrings. Jacob buried them beneath the terebinth that was by Shechem. As they decamped, the terror of God came upon the surrounding towns so that they did not chase down the sons of Jacob. Jacob came to Bethel and built there a menhir, and called the shrine El-of-Bethel, since there it was that God had revealed himself to him when he was fleeing his brother.

Rebecca's wet nurse Deborah died there and was buried just down from Bethel, beneath the oak thereafter called Oak-of-Weeping. Jacob set up a menhir at the shrine and poured out a libation on it and poured oil on it.

They left Bethel, and some way into the land they came to Ephrathah, where Rachel went into labor. She had a difficult labor, in the midst of which the midwife said to her, "Fear not, this one also will be a son for you." Rachel bore Benjamin. But she died and was buried on the way to Ephrathah, or Bethlehem. Jacob set up a menhir by her grave. That's the menhir of Rachel's grave to this day.

CHAPTER THREE

Joseph

Jacob traveled on back to Hebron. The lad Joseph was pasturing the flocks with his brothers. Jacob favored Joseph and made him a long-sleeved gown. His brothers saw that Joseph was their father's favorite and were jealous and hated him.[1]

Joseph dreamed a dream, and when he told it to his brothers, they hated him all the more. He said to them, "Listen to this dream I dreamed. We were out binding sheaves in the field when my sheaf rose up and even set itself up, while your sheaves surrounded my sheaf and bowed down to it."

His brothers said to him, "Are you planning to be king over us? Are you planning to rule us?" They hated him all the more for his dreams and his words.

He dreamed another dream, and told it to his brothers. "Listen, I dreamed another dream. It had the sun, the moon, and eleven stars bowing down to me." When he told it to his father and brothers, his father reproved him and said, "What is this dream you've had? Am I and your stepmother and your brothers to come and bow down to you to the ground?" His brothers were jealous of him, while his father kept his eye on the matter.

Joseph's brothers went to pasture the flocks near Shechem. Jacob sent Joseph to see how they were doing and to bring back word. Joseph found his brothers near Dothan. **They saw him in the distance, and** before he got too close to them, they plotted to kill him. **They said to one another, "There's that master of dreams over there, on his way**

---

1. At this point E began the insertions in J's history of Judah and Joseph. E's insertions were lengthy enough to turn the combined JE narrative into what it looks like today: the history of Joseph. This was Jeroboam I's intention.

here. Come on, let's kill him and throw him into one of the wells and say a wild animal ate him. Then we'll see what comes of his dreams."

Reuben listened, but determined to save Joseph from them. He said, "Let's not beat him to death." Reuben said to them, "Don't shed blood. Throw him into this well out here in the middle of nowhere, but don't lay a hand on him." This way he was hoping to save him and get him back to his father.

When Joseph got to his brothers, they stripped Joseph's cloak off him. They took him and threw him into the well, which was empty, without water in it. While they were eating, an Ishmaelite caravan came by. Judah proposed selling Joseph to the Ishmaelites. His brothers liked the idea. Some Midianite traders [from the caravan] passed close by, so they pulled Joseph up out of the well and sold Joseph to the Ishmaelites, and they took Joseph to Egypt.

Reuben [who had been elsewhere during the immediately preceding events] returned to the well. When he realized Joseph was not in the well, he tore his clothes and went back to the brothers and said, "The boy isn't there! Where can I turn now?"

They took Joseph's cloak and dipped it in goat's blood. They brought it back to their father and said, "We found this. Does it belong to your son?" He recognized it and said, "My son's cloak! An evil wild animal ate him! Joseph has been torn to pieces!" Jacob tore his coat, put sackcloth on, and mourned his son many days.

The Midianites sold Joseph in Egypt, to Potiphar, the officer of pharaoh, the captain of the bodyguard. Meanwhile, Judah got his daughter-in-law Tamar pregnant, and she bore two sons.

When Joseph was brought to Egypt, an Egyptian man—Potiphar, the officer of pharaoh, the captain of the bodyguard—bought him from the Ishmaelites who brought him down there. Yahweh was with Joseph, and the man's household prospered under Joseph's direction. Joseph was handsome. When the man's wife tried to seduce him, he refused, saying, "How shall I do this great evil, and break the law against God?" One time she got hold of his coat. When he fled without it, she cried out. When others came, she accused Joseph of trying to rape her. He was thrown into prison.

After these events, the cupbearer of the king of Egypt and the baker broke the law against their lord, the king of Egypt. Pharaoh became incensed with his two officers, the captain of the cupbearers and the captain of the bakers. He put them in the keep in the house of the captain of the bodyguard, in the roundhouse, where Joseph was being held captive. The captain of the bodyguard assigned Joseph to serve them.

After some time in the keep, the two men each had a dream during the same night, each with its own interpretation. When Joseph came to them in the morning, he looked at them and noticed they were vexed. He asked these officers to pharaoh who were with him in the keep of his lord's house, "Why are you looking bad today?"

They said to him, "We dreamed a dream, but there's no one to interpret it."

Joseph said to them, "Interpretations belong to God. Tell me your dreams."

The captain of the cupbearers told his dream to Joseph. "In my dream there was this vine in front of me. On the vine were three branches. As soon as it budded it blossomed, and its clusters ripened into grapes. Pharaoh's cup was in my hand, so I took the grapes and squeezed them into pharaoh's cup and placed the cup in pharaoh's hand."

Joseph said to him, "This is what it means. The three branches are three days. In three days pharaoh will lift up your head and return you to your post, and you will place pharaoh's cup in his hand as you used to do when you were his cupbearer. And if, when things are better for you, you remember that I was here with you, do me the kindness of bringing me to pharaoh's attention and so help me get out of this place. I was kidnapped from the land of the Hebrews, and I didn't do anything here, either, that would justify their putting me in the pit."

The captain of the bakers saw that Joseph gave a favorable interpretation and said to him, "I had a dream, too. There were these three baskets on my head. In the top basket was food for pharaoh, various kinds of baked goods. But birds were eating them out of the basket, off my head."

Joseph answered, "This is what it means. The three baskets are three days. In three days pharaoh will lift your head off you and have you impaled on a stake, and the birds will eat your flesh off you."

On the third day, which was pharaoh's birthday, he gave a feast for all his staff. With the whole court gathered, he lifted up the head of the captain of the cupbearers and the head of the captain of bakers. He returned the captain of the cupbearers to his service of cupbearing, and the captain placed pharaoh's cup in his hand. The captain of the bakers he had impaled. This was just as Joseph had said when he interpreted their dreams to them. The captain of the cupbearers, however, did not remember Joseph, but forgot him.

Two years later, pharaoh himself was having dreams. He was standing next to the Nile. Out of the Nile climbed seven handsome, fat cows, one after the other, and grazed in the reed grass. Then seven more cows climbed out of the Nile after them, repulsive and scrawny. These stood near the other cows on the bank of the Nile, and the repulsive, scrawny cows ate the seven handsome, fat cows—and pharaoh woke up.

He fell asleep again and had another dream. There were seven ears of grain on a single stalk, fat and handsome. And after them there were seven scrawny ears, blasted by the east wind and dried up. The scrawny ears swallowed up the seven fat and full ones—and pharaoh woke up, and it was just a dream.

In the morning he was bothered, so he summoned all the magicians and sages of Egypt. When pharaoh told them his dreams, none of them could interpret them for pharaoh. The captain of the cupbearers, however, said to pharaoh, "This day I am reminded of my sins. Some time ago when pharaoh became incensed with his officers, he stuck me in the keep in the house of the captain of the bodyguard, me and the captain of the bakers. One night he and I each had a dream, each with its own interpretation. With us there was a Hebrew boy, a servant of the chief of the bodyguard. When we told him, he interpreted our dreams for us, with a separate interpretation for each. And it turned out exactly as he had interpreted for us. Me you returned to my post, and him you had impaled."

Pharaoh sent for Joseph and had him rushed out of the pit. He shaved, changed clothes, and came into pharaoh's presence. Pharaoh said to Joseph, "I have had a dream, and there is no one to interpret it. But I heard tell about you that you could listen to a dream and interpret it."

Joseph answered, "It's not me. God will give pharaoh satisfaction."

Pharaoh said to Joseph, "In my dream, there I was, standing on the bank of the Nile, when up out of the Nile there came seven fat, handsomely formed cows that began to graze in the reed grass. Then seven more cows came up after them, meager and extremely scrawny and emaciated. I've never seen such awful-looking cows in all the land of Egypt. Then the emaciated and awful-looking cows ate the seven original fat cows. But when they landed in their bellies you couldn't tell they had landed in their bellies, because they looked as awful as before. Then I woke up.

"I had another dream, where there were seven handsome, full ears of grain on a single stalk. After them there were seven hardened, scrawny ears, blasted by the east wind and dried up. The scrawny ears swallowed up the seven handsome ears. I told it just this way to the magicians, but none of them could disclose its solution to me."

Joseph said to pharaoh, "Pharaoh has had but a single dream. What God is about to do he has disclosed to pharaoh. The seven handsome cows are seven years, and the seven handsome ears are seven years—you see, it is the same dream. The seven emaciated and awful-looking cows coming up after them are seven years, as are the seven sparse and wind-blasted ears. They represent seven years of famine. It is just what I told pharaoh: God has revealed to pharaoh what he is about to do. Seven years are about to come when there will be great abundance throughout the land of Egypt. Then after them, seven years of famine will take over. All the abundance in the land of Egypt will be forgotten, and the famine will devastate the land. No one will know anything about the abundance in the land because of the famine that's going to come afterward, since it is going to be an extremely severe famine. As for these years' appearing in pharaoh's dreams twice, that just means God has confirmed the matter, and that God is in a hurry to do it. Thus, let pharaoh look for a wise and discerning man to place in charge of the land of Egypt."

Joseph advised pharaoh to stockpile grain for seven years, and pharaoh liked the idea. **Pharaoh said to his officers, "Has there ever been a man like this one with the spirit of God in him?" Then he said to Joseph, "After God has informed you about all this, no one can match you for wisdom and discernment."**

Pharaoh appointed Joseph over all Egypt. Joseph married the daughter of the priest of Heliopolis. Joseph supervised the stockpiling of grain for seven years.

Joseph had two sons born to him before the first year of the famine. Asnat the daughter of Potiphera the priest of Heliopolis bore them to him. Joseph named the older Manasseh, **since "God has had me forget all the trouble I had in my father's household."** The second he named Ephraim, **since "God has made me fruitful in the land of my affliction."**

After seven years, the famine began. Pharaoh sent all his people to Joseph to buy food. As the famine became increasingly severe in Egypt and then over the whole earth, all the world came to Egypt to buy grain from Joseph. **When Jacob saw there was grain in Egypt, he said to his sons, "Why do you keep looking at each other? I hear there is grain in Egypt. Go down there and buy grain for us there, so we can live and not die."** So ten of Joseph's brothers went down to buy grain from Egypt. Jacob did not send Joseph's brother Benjamin with his brothers, for fear that some disaster might befall him.

The sons of Israel joined the throng making its way to Egypt. When they came to Joseph, he spoke harshly with them. "Where have you come from?" "From the land of Canaan," they said, "to buy food." Joseph recognized his brothers, but they did not recognize him. **And Joseph remembered the dreams he had dreamed about them,** and he said to them, "You are spies."

The brothers were unable to convince Joseph they were not spies. They said they were all there but the youngest. To test their honesty, Joseph insisted that only one be allowed to go back to fetch the youngest brother while the rest remained incarcerated. He kept them together in the guardhouse for three days. On the third day, Joseph said to them, "Do this if you want to live. **I fear God. If you are honest, let one of your brothers be kept in confinement in this house, and the rest of you** go, take famine stores back to your households. Then bring your youngest brother here, in order to verify your claims and not die."

They agreed to this. **They said to one another, "We are at fault because of our brother. We saw his dire distress when he begged mercy from us, but we refused. That's why this distress has come on us." Reuben answered them, "Didn't I tell you not to break the law against the boy? But you didn't listen. Now we are being made to pay for his blood." They didn't realize Joseph could understand them, since he was using an interpreter. Joseph turned away from them and wept, then returned to them and gave orders concerning them, and one of them, Simeon, was taken and bound before their eyes.**

Joseph sold them grain but had their money secretly put back in their satchels. When the brothers stopped for the night and discovered they still had their money, their hearts sank, **and trembling, they said to one another, "What is this God has done to us?"**

When they got back to **Jacob** their father in Canaan, they explained everything to him. "The lord of the land said to us, 'In this way I shall know that you are honest men: **leave one of your brothers here with me and** take famine stores for your households and go, bring your youngest brother to me, that I may know that you are not spies but honest men, so **I can give you back your brother** and you may move freely in the land.'" **And when they emptied their bags, and there was each man's money pouch in his bag, and they saw their money pouches, both they and their father were fearful.** Jacob their father said to them, "You have made me childless! Joseph is no more. Simeon is no more. And now you want to take away Benjamin. Everything is coming down on me." Reuben said to his father, "You may kill my two sons if I do not bring Benjamin back to you. Put him in my charge, and I shall return him to you."

Israel at first refused, but as the famine worsened, he gave in and sent the brothers off again to Egypt, with Judah responsible for Benjamin. When they arrived, Joseph summoned them. They were afraid he would arrest them for having stolen the money, so they approached the steward on the way in and explained the misunderstanding. "It's okay," he said. "Don't worry. Your god **and the God of your fathers** must have given you a little treasure in your bags. Your silver comes to me." **And he brought out Simeon to them,** then brought the men into Joseph's palace. When they came in, Joseph saw Benjamin. "Is this your youngest brother you were telling me about?" **And he said, "May God show you favor, my son,"** and then went quickly into a private room to get a grip on his emotions.

While the men feasted, Joseph again had the steward put their money back in their satchels, and his own silver goblet in Benjamin's satchel. When they had departed, the steward caught up with them and charged Benjamin with theft. Back in Joseph's presence, Judah spoke up on Benjamin's behalf. "What can we say to my lord? How can we respond, and how can we possibly put ourselves in the right? **God has uncovered your servants' wrongdoing.** We will be your slaves."

When Joseph declared that only Benjamin would be retained, Judah explained how he was responsible for Benjamin and made an ardent appeal to become Joseph's slave in Benjamin's stead. Joseph could control himself no longer. Ordering everyone else out of the room, he revealed himself to his brothers. **Joseph wept so loudly that some Egyptians heard, and it was found out in pharaoh's palace. Joseph said to his brothers, "I am Joseph. Is my father still alive?" But his brothers were unable to answer him because they were shaken with dismay by him.** Joseph said, "I am Joseph, whom you sold into Egypt. Don't be angry with yourselves for selling me to here. **It was for saving lives that God sent me ahead of you. The famine has lasted for two years so far in the midst of the earth, and there will be five more years when plowing will produce no harvest. God sent me ahead of you to provide you a remnant in the land and to save your lives through a great deliverance. So it wasn't you who sent me here, but God, in order to make me father to pharaoh, lord over his entire household and estate, and ruler over all Egypt.** Hurry back up to my father, and say to him, 'Thus says your son Joseph, "God has made me lord over all Egypt."' Bring your father and your families here to settle."

Then he fell on his brother Benjamin's neck and wept, while Benjamin wept on his neck. **He kissed all his brothers and wept over them. Afterward, as his brothers were speaking to him, word got to** pharaoh's palace: "Joseph's brothers have come." Pharaoh and his officers were pleased with this. Pharaoh told Joseph to have his brothers bring their father and families to settle in Egypt.

They went up from Egypt and came in the land of Canaan to Jacob, their father. They told him, "Joseph is still alive. Indeed, he is ruler over all the land of Egypt." Jacob's heart sank, because he didn't believe them. They told him all Joseph's instructions that he had given to them. When he saw the carts Joseph had sent to transport him, the spirit of Jacob, their father, came alive. Israel said, "That's it. If Joseph is alive, I have to go see him before I die."

Israel decamped with everything he owned. When he arrived at Beersheba, he made sacrifices to the God of his father Isaac. In visions in the night, God said, "Jacob, Jacob." And he said, "Right here." And he said, "I am El, the God of your father. Do not be afraid to go down to Egypt, because I am going to make you a great nation there. I shall go down with you to Egypt, and I shall also bring you up, and Joseph shall place his hands over your eyes."

Jacob got up and left Beersheba. The Israelites brought Jacob, their father, and their children and wives in the carts pharaoh had sent to transport them. They took their livestock with everything they had in the land of Canaan and came to Egypt, Jacob and all his offspring with him. They arrived in Egypt, were reunited with Joseph, and assigned by pharaoh to settle in Goshen as herders. Pharaoh said to Joseph, "Have them settle in Goshen. And if you know among them any strong men, appoint them as livestock captains over the flocks and herds belonging to me."

Joseph brought Jacob, his father, and had him stand in the presence of pharaoh. Jacob blessed pharaoh. Pharaoh said to Jacob, "How many are the years of your life?" Jacob said to pharaoh, "The years of my wayfaring are one hundred and thirty. Meager and bad have the years of my life been, not to be compared with the years of the lives of my ancestors, in the time of their wayfaring." Jacob blessed pharaoh and left his presence. Joseph settled his father and brothers and gave them tenure in the land of Egypt, on good land.

Joseph made sure his family were fed, along with the rest of the Egyptians. When it was time for Israel to die, he summoned Joseph and made him swear to bury him in Canaan. Joseph swore to him, and Israel bowed at the head of the bed.

Some time after, Joseph was told, "Your father is ill." So he took his two sons with him, Manasseh and Ephraim. It was told Jacob, "Your son Joseph has come to you." Israel started to bless the boys but got his right and left hand crossed. Then he blessed Joseph in these words: "May God, in whose presence my ancestors Abram and Isaac steadfastly walked, the God who shepherded me all my life to this day, the genie who redeemed me from every evil, bless the boys, and let them be called by my name and the name of my ancestors Abram and Isaac, and let them spawn abundantly in the midst of the land."

Joseph noticed Israel had his hands crossed and tried to straighten them out, but Israel refused to change them. So he blessed Ephraim ahead of Manasseh. Then Israel said to Joseph, "As I am about to die, may God be with you, and bring you back to the land of your ancestors. I hereby grant you Shechem, as a man equal to your brothers." Then Israel blessed each of his twelve sons.

Israel died and was mourned in Egypt. Then Joseph led a major expedition to Canaan to bury his father there.

When their father died, Joseph's brothers became fearful, as they thought, "Suppose Joseph holds a grudge against us. He would be sure to pay us back all the evil we have brought him." So they instructed Joseph, "Before your father died he instructed us as follows: 'Tell Joseph, by all means forgive your brothers' transgression and violations of the law in bringing evil to you.' So forgive the transgression of the servants of your father's God."

Joseph wept as they spoke to him. His brothers even went to him and fell before him and said, "Here we are, your slaves." Joseph said to them, "Do not be afraid. Should I take the place of God? You devised evil against me, but God devised that the same should be good, to achieve what he has today, saving the lives of a great people. So now, do not be afraid. I will take care of you and your sons." Thus he consoled them and addressed them kindly.

Joseph returned to Egypt with his father's household and lived for one hundred and ten years. Joseph saw Ephraim's grandchildren, and even when the sons of Machir, the son of Manasseh, were born, they were placed on Joseph's knees.

Joseph said to his brothers, "I am about to die. May God attend to you without fail and bring you up from this land, to the land he swore to Abram, Isaac, and Jacob." And Joseph made the Israelites swear when he said, "When God attends you without fail, bring up my bones from here." Joseph died, and they embalmed him and placed him in a coffin in Egypt.

CHAPTER FOUR

Horeb

After the pharaoh who promoted Joseph died, the descendants of Israel lost their land tenure and were pressed into forced labor, building grain storage facilities for the new pharaoh. Conditions for the Israelite slaves were extremely harsh.

The king of Egypt said to the Hebrew midwives, one of whom was named Shiprah and the other, Puah, "When you assist the Hebrew women in giving birth, and you look at the birth stones, if it is a boy, then put him to death, but if it is a girl, let her live." But the midwives feared God and did not do as the king of Egypt had ordered them to. Instead they let the boys live. The king of Egypt summoned the midwives and said to them, "Why are you doing this, letting the boys live? The midwives said to pharaoh, "Because the Hebrew women are not like the Egyptian women. They are alive! Before the midwife gets to them, they have already given birth."

God treated the midwives well. The people multiplied and became extremely strong. And because the midwives feared God, he provided them with sons. Pharaoh therefore commanded all his court, "Any son born to the Hebrews throw into the Nile, but any girl you may let live."

A man from the household of Levi went and took a Levite daughter. The woman got pregnant and gave birth to a son. She saw that he was a good baby, so concealed him for three months. When she was unable to conceal him any longer, she got for him a reed basket, smeared it with bitumen and pitch, placed the boy in it, and placed it among the reeds on the bank of the Nile. His sister placed herself at a distance to find out what would happen to him.

The daughter of pharaoh came down to the Nile to bathe, while her maids walked by the side of the river. She saw the basket among the reeds and sent her servant to get it. When she opened it, she saw him, the boy. The tyke began to cry, and she took pity on him. When she said, "It must be a Hebrew boy," his sister said to pharaoh's daughter, "Shall I go and call a wet nurse for you from the Hebrew women, so she can nurse the boy for you?" Pharaoh's daughter said to her, "Go ahead."

The girl went and called the boy's mother. Pharaoh's daughter said to her, "Take this boy and nurse him for me, and I will pay you for it." The woman took the boy and nursed him. When he had grown bigger, she brought him to pharaoh's daughter, and he became her son. She named him Moses, saying, "After all, I drew him out of the water."

At that time, when Moses had grown up, he was out among his kin and observed an Egyptian beating a Hebrew. After checking that they were alone, he beat the Egyptian to death. Word got back to pharaoh, and Moses had to flee into the desert. There he chanced to meet the daughters of the priest of Midian and ended up marrying one of them.

Years later, after that pharaoh had died, Moses was out pasturing the flock of **his father-in-law Jethro**, the priest of Midian. He had led the flock some ways into the desert **and come to the mountain of God, Horeb**. The genie of Yahweh appeared to him in a fiery flame out of a bush. When Moses saw that the bush was burning but that the bush did not burn up, he said, "I must go over and see this remarkable sight. Why isn't the bush burning?"

When Yahweh saw he was coming over to see, **God called out to him from the midst of the bush, "Moses, Moses!"** He said, "Right here." Yahweh said, "Do not come near here. Remove your sandals from your feet, for the place at which you are standing is sanctified ground. I am the God of your ancestor, the God of Abram, the God of Isaac, and the God of Jacob."

Moses hid his face because he was afraid to look at God.

"I have seen fully the oppression of my people in Egypt. I have heard their outcry in the face of their slave drivers, for I know their pain. I have come down to rescue them from the hand of Egypt and to bring them up from that land to a good land. So now, since the outcry of the Israelites has reached me, and moreover I have seen the affliction with which the Egyptians afflict them, now go. I'm going to send you to pharaoh. Bring my people the Israelites out of Egypt."

Moses said to God, "Who am I that I should go to pharaoh, or that I should bring the Israelites out of Egypt?"

He said, "But I will be with you. And this will be a sign for you that I have sent you: when you have brought the people out of Egypt, you all shall serve God at this mountain."

Moses said to God, "Look, supposing I go to the Israelites and say to them, 'The God of your ancestors has sent me to you,' and they say to me, 'What's his name?' What am I going to say to them?"

God said to Moses, "I will be what I will be [namely, with you]." And he said, "Thus you shall say to the Israelites: 'I-Will-Be sent me to you.'" And God said further to Moses, "Thus you shall say to the Israelites: 'Yahweh, the God of your ancestors, the God of Abram, the God of Isaac, and the God of Jacob, sent me to you.' This is my name forever, and this is the way you should commemorate me for all generations to come. Gather the Israelite sheikhs, and tell them Yahweh is going to deliver them. They will listen to you, and you can all go to pharaoh and tell him you want to go for three days into the desert to serve me."

Moses said, "They're not going to believe this, and they're not going to listen to me."

Yahweh gave Moses some signs he could perform to convince the Israelite leaders. Moses resisted, but Yahweh overcame his resistance. He sent him off with final instructions.

So Moses went and returned to Jethro, his father-in-law. He said to him, "I want to go and return to my brothers who are in Egypt, so that I can see whether they are still living." Jethro said to Moses, "Go safely."

While Moses was in Midian, Yahweh said to Moses, "Go back to Egypt. All the men seeking your life are dead." So Moses took his wife and sons and put them on asses and returned to the land of Egypt.

Moses made his request to pharaoh, which made pharaoh all the meaner. He only worsened the condition of the Israelites. Yahweh had Moses turn the Nile to blood and produce a plague of frogs, then flies and pestilence. When Yahweh made an extremely severe hailstorm, pharaoh said, "You are right, and we are in the wrong. Entreat Yahweh. We have had enough thunder of God and hail. I will let you go."

Moses said to him, "Just out of the city, I will spread my hands toward Yahweh. The thunder and hail will cease, so that you may know that Yahweh owns the earth. And as for you and your servants, I know that you will still not fear God."

The hail stopped, but after that Moses brought on locusts, darkness, and the death of all firstborn. When even these failed to change pharaoh's mind, Yahweh rescued them out of Egypt, and they fled by night.

When pharaoh had let the people go, God did not lead them by the road to the land of the Philistines, even though it was the shortest, because God said, "The people may change their minds when

they see battle, and go back to Egypt." God turned the people to the
way to the desert, by way of Sup Sea. As the Israelites went up from
the land with excitement, Moses took Joseph's bones with him.
Joseph had made the Israelites swear when he said, "When God
without fail attends you, bring up my bones from here with you."

Yahweh went in front of the people during the day in a cloud pillar
and during the night in a fire pillar. Neither pillar ever left its place in
front of the people.

Pharaoh chased the people in chariots. The people looked back and
became extremely frightened. They said to Moses, "Were there no
graves in Egypt that you had to bring us to the desert to die?" Moses
replied, "Don't be afraid. Just stand there and see the liberation of
Yahweh. Yahweh will fight for you."

**The genie of God, who had been going before the camp of Israel,
went behind them.** The cloud pillar moved from their front to their
rear and positioned itself between the camp of Egypt and the camp of
Israel. During the night Yahweh frightened Egypt into the sea, and
they drowned. Moses led Israel from there into the desert.

Jethro the priest of Midian, Moses' father-in-law, heard **all that
God had done for Moses and for Israel his people**, that Yahweh had
brought Israel out of Egypt. Moses' father-in-law, **Jethro,** took Moses'
wife Zipporah with her belongings and her two sons, of whom the first
was named Gershom because he said, "I was a resident alien in a
foreign land," and the second Eliezer because "the God of my father
was my help and saved me from the sword of pharaoh." Then **Jethro,**
Moses' father-in-law, and Moses' sons and wife came to Moses in the
desert where he was encamped, **at the mountain of God.** He said to
Moses, "I am your father-in-law, **Jethro,** who have come to you, along
with your wife and her two sons." Moses went out to meet his father-
in-law, greeted him, invited him into his tent, and told him everything
that had happened since he had last seen him.

Jethro was glad to hear about it. He blessed Yahweh and proclaimed
how great he was. **Then Jethro, Moses' father-in-law, took a whole
burnt offering and other sacrifices for God, and all the sheikhs of
Israel gathered to eat food with the father-in-law of Moses in the
presence of God.**

The next day, Moses took his seat to pass judgment for the people.
The people stayed with Moses from morning until evening. Moses'
father-in-law saw everything he was doing for the people and said,
"What is this you are doing for the people? Why do you take your
seat alone, with all the people standing with you from morning until
evening?" Moses said to his father-in-law, "Because the people come

to me to make inquiry of God. Whenever they have a case at law they come to me, and I pass judgment between the litigants and thus inform them regarding the statutes of God and his laws."

Moses' father-in-law said to him, "What you are doing is not good. Both you and these people with you are extremely foolish. The matter is too burdensome for you. You cannot do it alone. Take my advice. May God be with you, and you yourself be the people's intermediary with God. Bring the cases to God, then admonish them regarding the statutes and laws. Then may you look for men of means, ability, and influence from among all the people, men who fear God, men who value truth in testimony and who despise bribes. Appoint these over the people, as chiefs of groups of a thousand, chiefs of groups of a hundred, chiefs of groups of fifty, and chiefs of groups of twenty. Let them pass judgment for the people under ordinary circumstances. If there is a particularly weighty case, they may bring that to you. But as for all the lesser cases, let them pass judgment themselves. Make things lighter for yourself, and let them bear some of the burden. If you do as I advise, and God continues to pass on orders to you, then you will be able to last, and all these people, moreover, will go to their homes with justice and peace."

Moses took his father-in-law's advice and did everything he said. Moses selected men of means, ability, and influence from all Israel and made them heads over the people, chiefs of groups of a thousand, chiefs of groups of a hundred, chiefs of groups of fifty, and chiefs of groups of twenty. As a rule, they would pass judgment for the people. The difficult cases they brought to Moses, but all the minor cases they passed judgment on themselves.

Moses then sent his father-in-law off, and he traveled back to his homeland. Israel came to the desert of Sinai and camped in that desert, in front of the mountain. **Moses went up to God**, and Yahweh said to Moses, "I will come to you in a cloud, so the people can hear me speak with you, so they will trust you. Go to the people and sanctify them today and tomorrow. Have them wash their garments and get ready on the day after tomorrow, for on the third day Yahweh will come down, in view of all the people, onto the mountain of Sinai. Bound off this mountain on all sides from the people. Then when the horn sounds, let them come up to the mountain."

Moses went down and sanctified the people. On the day after the morrow, as morning came, there were thunder and lightning, and a heavy cloud over the mountain. **The sound of the shofar got louder and louder, and all the people in the camp trembled. Moses led out the people from the camp to meet God, and they positioned themselves at** the foot of the mountain. The whole of the mountain at Sinai began to smoke as Yahweh came down on it as fire. The smoke went up like smoke from a furnace. While the whole mountain shook severely and the sound of the shofar got louder still, Moses spoke and God answered him through the sound.

Yahweh came down and summoned Moses to the top of the mountain. Yahweh charged Moses to warn the people, even the priests, not to break through to see him. Moses assured him bounds had been set and then went back down to the people.

When all the people saw the thunderings and lightning and the sound of the shofar and the mountain smoking, the people feared and shook and stayed at a distance. They said to Moses, "You speak with us so we can hear, but let God not speak with us, or we will die." Moses said to the people, "Do not be afraid. God has come to test you, and so that fear of him will be before you so you will not break the law." So the people stood at a distance, while Moses approached the heavy cloud where God was.

Then Yahweh said to Moses, "Thus you shall say to the Israelites: 'Having seen that I have spoken with you all from the sky, you shall not make like me gods of silver or gods of gold. Instead, make an altar of earth for me and thereon sacrifice your whole burnt offerings and community meal offerings, your flocks and herds. In every sanctuary where I have my name addressed, I will come to you and bless you. If you insist on making an altar out of stones, never make it out of hewn stones; if you strike any part of it with an iron tool, you will profane it. And you shall not go up on my altar by steps, so that your nakedness will not be uncovered on it.'

"The following are the case rulings you shall set before them:

"When you buy a Hebrew slave, he shall work for six years. In the seventh year he shall depart a free man, without having to make any payment. If he arrives single, he shall depart single. If he has a wife, his wife shall depart with him. If his master gives him a wife and she bears him sons or daughters, the wife and her children shall belong to her master, and the slave shall depart single. If the slave states plainly, 'I love my master, my wife, and my sons; I choose not to depart a free man,' then his master shall have him approach God and have him approach the door or doorpost, and his master shall pierce his ear with an awl, and he shall work for him for life.

"When a man sells his daughter as a slave, she shall not depart free the way the manslaves depart. If she displeases her master and he has not designated her [as a wife for someone in his family], he shall effect her ransom.[1] He does not have the power to sell her outside the immediate extended family, since he violated her rights. If he designates her for his son, he shall treat her according to the rules applying to daughters. If he takes another wife, he shall not withhold from the first her meat, her clothing, or her oil ration. If he fails to provide these three things for her, she shall depart without having to make any payment, with no money transaction.

"Whoever beats a man to death shall be put to death. If he was not on the hunt for him, but God occasioned that he fell into his hand, I shall designate for you a shrine to which he may flee. If, however, a man presumes to murder his fellow with cunning, you shall take him away from my altar to be put to death. Whoever beats his father or mother shall be put to death. Whoever commits kidnapping shall be put to death, whether he sells him or still has him when caught.

"When men have a fight and one beats the other with a rock or his fist so that he is laid up but does not die, if he can get up and walk about in the village with the help of his staff, the one who beat him shall be cleared, except that he must compensate him for his lost time and see to his complete recovery. When a man strikes his male or female slave with a club so that he or she dies on the spot, the death shall be avenged by death by the community at large. If he or she lasts a day or two, the death is not to be avenged, since after all the slave represented the master's own money. When men have a fight and injure a pregnant woman so that she suffers a miscarriage but there is no harm to herself, a fine shall be paid by one of the men according to what the woman's husband shall demand, to be paid according to the reckoning of the fetus's age. If the woman herself suffers harm, you shall pay a life in place of a life, an eye in place of an eye, a tooth in place of a tooth, a hand in place of a hand, a foot in place of a foot, a burn in place of a burn, a bruise in place of a bruise, a blow in place of a blow. When a man strikes the eye of his male or female slave and ruins it, he shall let him or her go a free person in compensation for the eye. If he knocks out the tooth of his male or female slave, he shall let him or her go a free person in compensation for the tooth.

"When an ox gores a man or a woman to death, the ox shall be stoned, and its flesh shall not be eaten, and the owner of the ox shall be free of liability. If the ox is in the habit of goring and has done so previously, and its owner has been warned but has not taken precautions with it, and it kills a man or woman, the ox shall be stoned and

1. Adrian Schenker, "Affranchissement d'une esclave selon Ex 21, 7–11," *Biblica* 69 (1988): 547–56.

its owner also put to death. If the magistrate assigns a ransom to him, he may make payment for his life, as long as it is the entire amount assigned. If it gores a son or daughter, it shall be dealt with according to this ruling. If the ox gores a male or female slave, its owner shall pay the slave's master thirty shekels of silver, and the ox shall be stoned.

"When a man opens a well or digs a well and in either case fails to cover it again, and an ox or an ass falls in, the owner of the well shall give compensation. He shall render money to its owner, and the dead animal shall belong to him.

"When the ox of one man injures the ox of another so that it dies, they shall sell the surviving ox and split the proceeds, and shall divide the dead ox between them as well. If it is known that the ox was in the habit of goring and had done so previously, and its owner had not taken precautions with it, he shall give full compensation—an ox in place of the ox—and the dead ox shall be all his.

"When a man steals an ox or sheep and slaughters it or sells it, he shall make compensation in the amount of five head of cattle for an ox, or four sheep or goats for a sheep. If the thief is caught in the act and beaten to death, there is no bloodguilt involved. But if he escapes until daylight and is then beaten, there is bloodguilt. The thief shall make full restitution. If he lacks the means, he shall be sold for the value of what he stole. If what he stole is found in his possession, whether an ox or ass or sheep, he shall restore two animals for each one stolen.

"When a man is burning over a field or vineyard, if he lets the fire spread so that it burns the field of another, he shall make restitution with the best produce of his own field or the best produce of his own vineyard. When the fire is spreading, if it catches on brushwood, so that shocked grain or standing grain or the field itself is burned up, the one who started the fire shall make full restitution.

"When a man gives money or articles to another for safekeeping, and anything thus rendered is stolen from the latter's house, if the thief is found, he shall make twofold restitution. If the thief is not found, the owner of the house shall be brought to God, to declare under oath that he himself did not lay hands on the other's property. In every case involving misappropriation—whether of an ox, an ass, a sheep, a piece of clothing, or anything that has gone missing—about which someone claims, 'Hey, that's mine,' both parties shall present their case before God. The one whom God convicts shall make twofold restitution to the other. When a man gives an ass, an ox, a sheep, or any other beast for safekeeping, and it dies, is injured, or is snatched away while no one is watching, the custodian shall take an oath by God[2] that he did not lay hands on the other's property. The owners must accept this, and no restitution shall be made. But if he did steal from him, he shall make restitution to the owners. If it has been torn up by a wild animal, he shall bring it as evidence. For any animal thus torn up he shall not make restitution.

"When a man borrows an animal from another, if it is injured or dies and its owners are not with it, he shall make full restitution. If he is a hired worker, it will come out of his wage.

"When a man seduces a virgin who is not engaged and has intercourse with her, he shall pay her marriage price and marry her. If her father refuses to let him marry her, he shall pay him in silver the customary marriage price for virgins."

Yahweh told Moses to come up the mountain with the leaders and sheikhs of Israel, then approach Yahweh by himself. They all went up, and they saw the god of Israel. Yahweh did not strike out at these chiefs of Israel, even though they saw God, and they ate and drank. Moses got up, and Moses went up to the mountain of God.

Moses led the Israelites through several adventures in the desert until they arrived at the edge of Israel, where the oracle Balaam blessed them and cursed their worst enemies.

2. The traditional Hebrew text has *yahweh*. The Greek manuscripts all have *theos*, representing *'elohim*.

CHAPTER FIVE
Solomon's Tyranny

E was written in defense of the revolution that overthrew the house of David in Israel. Because Solomon's rule fomented the revolution, that is where an understanding of E begins.[1]

THE SUCCESSION

As head of the house of David over the united states of Judah and Israel, David amassed enormous power and wealth and died in bed. The succession, which became an issue before he died, was disorderly. Custom favored David's oldest surviving son, Adonijah, the fourth son of six born in Hebron. Adonijah had the backing of the heads of tribal military and cultic forces, Joab and Abiathar. He put on an enormous feast at the lower end of the royal gardens outside Jerusalem's eastern wall. He invited his brothers and the officials of his father's palace and expected them to anoint him king before going home.

One royal son, according to his own account, stayed away. Solomon, born tenth in line to the throne, declared that David had named him successor. To back himself up, Solomon had Benaiah and Zadok, David's long-time henchmen and the chiefs of David's personal military guard and cult; Nathan, a compliant palace oracle; and Solomon's mother, Bathsheba, who bested the rest of the harem. After confirming the appointment with David, as later related, Solomon's party called out the Aegean guard, David's old mercenary

1. For the history of Solomon's reign, see J. Maxwell Miller and John H. Hayes, *A History of Ancient Israel and Judah* (Philadelphia: Westminster, 1986), 189–217; E. W. Heaton, *Solomon's New Men: The Emergence of Ancient Israel as a Nation State* (New York: Pica, 1974); Robert R. Stieglitz, "Long-Distance Seafaring in the Ancient Near East," *Biblical Archaeologist* 47 (1984): 134–42; the entire double issue of the *Bulletin of the American Schools of Oriental Research* 277/278 (1990).

retinue, and conducted their own coronation at the upper end of the royal gardens, within earshot of the festivities at the lower end.

At the completion of ceremonies, King Solomon rode David's mule back up into the fortress, with his armed guard in his wake marching boisterously to trumpets, pipes, and drums. Adonijah's party broke up, and his supporters faded away. Adonijah made quick work of doing obeisance to his new master, who for a time spared his life. Solomon's other brothers followed Adonijah's example.

The royal succession was thus determined by a palace coup. The successful party was one whose ties to the tribes of Israel were practically nonexistent. Solomon was a youth, utterly unknown to the people, and powerless on his own. His Negeb and Aegean toughs, unentangled in tribal alliances, factions, and networks, used Solomon to complete their takeover of Israel in the name of David. Bathsheba was eager to cooperate. Her father, Eliam, was one of David's troop, as had been her husband, Uriah. Eliam's father was Ahitophel, who, disgraced by David's murder of Uriah and taking of Bathsheba, supported Absalom but ended his life in suicide. Bathsheba, a daughter of the village Giloh, and her son put themselves in the hands of palace friends looking for a royal tool.

Solomon, leveraged by David's cronies, a youth of the purple whose horizons reached little beyond the city of his birth, had overthrown popular custom. Under David the institutions of tribe and state had rudely meshed. At David's death, the state took over. Solomon's reign was stamped from the start by the suppression of two hundred years of political and social relations in the highlands. Tutored by Benaiah, young Solomon faulted his father for being irresolute and ordered Adonijah and Joab murdered. Abiathar he banished to house arrest in Anathoth, a village north of Jerusalem. When all this was accomplished, Solomon's scribe rewrote David's apologia on Saul and Absalom to show that kindness to tribal forces produced turmoil, that Solomon was destined at birth to succeed to the throne, and that the brutality necessary for this end was but obedience to the great David himself.[2] History was now on his side.

SOLOMON'S REIGN

The Bible says Solomon ruled forty years. Like some other parts of the description of Solomon's reign, that number looks legendary. But because Solomon, like David, apparently died without help, it cannot

---

2. P. Kyle McCarter, Jr., "'Plots, True or False': The Succession Narrative as Court Apologetic," *Interpretation* 35 (1981): 355–67.

be far off. The opulence of Solomon's court was legendary. Solomon was never permitted, however, to develop his father's prowess, and the trade and territory he ruled never sufficed to support his taste in force and fun. The Philistine buffer with Egypt was weakened during David's reign, and the Negeb tribesmen were pliable and thus not always loyal. Egypt overran Solomon's western border early in his reign and controlled the coastal plain at least as far north as Gezer. Partly at Egypt's instigation, the empire began to crumble a bit at a time. At Solomon's death his kingdom imploded, and his son was left to rule over Judah alone, roughly the territory ruled by David from Hebron. The house of David had come full circle in less than two generations.

David's army had been economical. Its mobile professional core was deployed for quick strikes from Jerusalem. David inherited many of his lowland garrisons from the Philistines, and they required little modification. His chariot corps was small. The tribal infantry supported itself through normal subsistence. Although the system of villager impoverishment was put in place in the highlands in David's day, at that time the voluntary tribal infantry still hung together, so the villagers did not lose all advantage. As long as villagers played some role in the military, they could ward off ruination. Tradition had it that David and Joab failed, however, to institute the census they thought necessary to regularize the tribal draft. As David's reign progressed, the tribal military and its commander Joab became increasingly expendable.

Solomon's military was organized on a basis more reminiscent of the Egyptian New Kingdom in Palestine than of David's army: chariot corps, large standing army, and necessary apparatus. The elite Aegean palace guard remained on duty, but its role in patrolling the empire was replaced by a standing army of charioteers (who specialized in lowland fighting), mercenaries, and drafted infantry. The standing army's function was ostensibly defensive, but the tax system supporting it was offensive, against Palestinian villagers. Villagers' interests had long since ceased to be defended. They were pressed ever harder to provide the means of their own oppression. As Solomon's empire gradually disintegrated and his Palestinian villagers were exhausted trying to cover the costs of his imperial military, Solomon's defense budget fattened into a sustained deficit.

In the course of his reign, Solomon employed the corvée under Adoram to refortify cities along the lowland trade route through the realm. These were Hazor, Megiddo, Gezer, Lower Beth Horon, and Baalath, along with Tamar in the Arabah. They were equipped as storage depots for local produce and stabling centers for the chariotry that operated out of them. The monumental six-chambered city gates of Hazor, Megiddo, and Gezer were built on a uniform plan. Large above-ground storehouses dating from Solomon's time, consisting of ranks of long, narrow rooms with thick walls and foundations, have been discovered in Jericho, Lachish, Megiddo, Bethshemesh, and possibly T. Jemmeh and T. Beit-Mirsim. For the first time, political Israel possessed cities, with their accompanying temples, military palaces, administrative chambers, and oversized granaries.

The size and cost of Solomon's corps were staggering.[3] Chariots cost 600 shekels each and trained horses, 150 shekels. Each vehicle required three horses, so chariot and team came to 1,050 shekels. Then there were the accessory costs: crews, maintenance personnel, weapons, spare parts, housing for personnel, storage areas and repair shops, stables, and fodder. Frequent disassembly and lubrication with olive oil were essential. The corps thus consumed a large quantity of the basic foodstuffs of Palestine. The horses required months of training, then ongoing practice and grooming by skilled personnel. Solomon's chariots numbered 1,400; horses, 4,000; and crews and support staff, up to 12,000—all supported on food grown by others. The chariot army all told required an outlay on the order of 1,470,000 shekels, leaving aside the expense of upkeep and renewal.

How much was a million and a half shekels? A generation later, a slave was valued at 30 shekels. On this basis, an equipped chariot was worth between 35 and 50 slaves. The entire corps represented the equivalent of a half-million to a million rams, or several rams for every man, woman, and child in Israel. This did not include the 3,650 oxen, 7,300 cattle, 36,500 lambs, and tons of wheat and beans required to provision Solomon's court in Jerusalem. Solomon's colossal tax in kind was matched by a monstrous tax in work. To build fortresses, palaces, and the temple, Solomon required a crew of 30,000 stout men and youth, deployed in battalions of 10,000 each for a month at a time— with two months off at home—for cutting, hauling, and shipping timber in Lebanon. Solomon drafted 80,000 stonecutters and 70,000 basket carriers for forced labor. The staff that kept this army of workers at their tasks numbered 3,300. These scores of thousands were fed from state stores or forced to bring food from home stores. Other work could be done only by skilled craftspeople from the cities of the Phoenician coast, who required hire and feeding.

3. The description and figures that follow were developed by Chris Hauer, "The Economics of National Security in Solomonic Israel," *Journal for the Study of the Old Testament* 18 (1980): 63–73.

The centerpiece of Solomon's building program was the palace and temple in Jerusalem. David had commandeered Jerusalem's best house and fixed it up, but that was not good enough for his successor. David's household cult had been conducted, as far as is known, in a tent in Jerusalem, unless in an existing small temple with little or no renovation. That was not good enough, either. By Solomon's fourth year, Adoram had expanded the state corvée and put it to work on a new house for Solomon and a magnificent new or renovated house for Yahweh. Solomon's house took thirteen years to build and Yahweh's seven. Both were constructed out of finely hewn stone and delicately carved cedar and cypress paneling and adornment, and both contained quantities of gold, silver, and bronze. The temple was built at the north end of the city of David. The city lay on a rocky spur protected on three sides by abrupt ravines. The north, where it merged with a plateau, was its weak side. If tradition is true, David or Solomon expropriated the threshing floor on the exposed plateau from a resident Hurrian for the construction of the fortress temple, whose precinct completed the city's defenses. The loss of the threshing floor signaled the termination of food production by the city populace themselves; the city was taken over by the government, the king's greater household. One estimate has put the number of officials and staff in Jerusalem at sixteen hundred and their families at another four thousand.

The temple was designed by Phoenician craftspeople on the Palestinian-Syrian pattern of the time for temples of urban gods. It was derived from the megaron, or long-room, style attested in northern Syria for several hundred years before Solomon and widespread in the eastern Mediterranean region outside of Egypt for much of the second millennium B.C.E. The architecture, outfitting, procedure, and ideology of Solomon's cult of Yahweh were indistinguishable from cults of Baal and equivalent deities throughout northern Palestine, Syria, and the Phoenician coast. (Temples built in other Judahite and Israelite cities during Solomon's reign, such as at Arad in the far south of Judah, may have been modeled more according to contemporary highland house architecture.) Two free-standing pillars before the entrance announced in stone the security of the dynastic succession and its beneficence. The only object pertaining to tribal Israel was its portable battle chest, which was deposited in the innermost sanctuary, between two gigantic winged guardian figures (cherubim) of Syrian design, and never used or seen again. This house of Yahweh was for the private use of the king and senior priests. Except for those who helped complete it, most Israelites scarcely laid eyes on it, much less worshiped Yahweh in it.

David's mate and Solomon's promoter, Zadok, established the state priesthood of Jerusalem. The temple endowment included prebends from David's conquered territory. These had a tendency to turn into hereditary grants. As the military grew and the imperial territory shrank, the state made successive incursions on highland Israelite lands to provide for priestly servants. Both military and priesthood were dominated by Judahites and aliens, reflecting the makeup of David's forces. At the temple, David's prayer service was carried on as before, but given a far more elaborate setting, including especially the slaughter of animals on a regal scale and the incineration, roasting, or boiling of their flesh to propitiate Yahweh and feed the priests. The court's daily rations were adequate and far in excess of the quantities of meat consumed in the villages. It was said that at the dedication of the temple, an occasion for an unusual feast, the priests slaughtered 22,000 oxen and 120,000 sheep. The new temple meant meat for everyone, for one day. The hardship of oxen lost to village use and the increased cost of finding an ox for the next plowing are difficult to imagine. In time, Zadok followed his contemporary David to the grave. His son Azariah succeeded to his office, land tenure, and income.

Other court offices became hereditary, along with their endowments. Another son of Zadok was made a commissar. Two sons of David's chief scribe succeeded to his office. One of them may have had an Egyptian element in his name, carrying on the family heritage. David's oracle Nathan, whose indispensable pronouncements on Solomon's legitimacy assured his place in the court executive, did well by his sons. One had charge of the commissariat, a position with vast responsibility in a regime like Solomon's. Another became a priest and national security adviser. Benaiah endured as commander-in-chief to old age. The name of his successor is not recorded. Benaiah was outdone in longevity by Adoram, whose management of the state corvée extended from David to Solomon's son Rehoboam. Ahishar, an apparent newcomer, was placed in charge of the king's estates and enterprises. In a sense, Solomon became too legendary. A better sense of Solomon's rule could be had by recalling not Solomon himself but the aging quadrumvirate—Zadok, Benaiah, Nathan, and Adoram—who elevated him and wrote his scripts.

In Jerusalem each day, Solomon's men ate thirty sacks of flour; sixty sacks of meal; ten fat oxen; twenty pasture-fed oxen; a hundred sheep; assorted harts, gazelles, roebucks, and fowl; and unspecified quantities of wine and oil. This menu may look exaggerated, but it is probably more or less accurate. It was Nathan's son Azariah's job to make sure this food was on the table. Azariah organized the commissariat, the office for taxation and royal provision, along Egyptian lines, as David probably had Judah. Azariah divided Israel into twelve districts, each ruled by a commissar responsible for provisions in Jerusalem for one month and for the chariot horses in his own district on a continual basis. Judah retained its districts as under David, apparently with its own thirteenth commissar. Whether Israel was taxed more heavily than Judah under this arrangement, as often suggested, is unclear, but likely.

Azariah discarded David's tribal policy for Israel and designed most of the districts not to match traditional territories of the tribes of Israel, thus voiding the tribes as a basis of state administration.[4] Through these districts Azariah and Benaiah instituted the state military draft David had failed to arrange, and through them Adoram ran his parallel, and no doubt overlapping, state labor draft. As Solomon grew increasingly unable to afford his imperial chariotry and mercenaries and turned increasingly to the district draft, he laid the ground for a resurgence of peasant advantage after his death. The commissars tended to be king's men rather than local or tribal leaders. Zadok's son Ahimaaz, a royal son-in-law, was stationed in charge of Hazor and surroundings. This assignment put him way out of his family's home area. Baana, the son of David's security adviser Hushai and another of Solomon's sons-in-law, from southwest of Bethel, served in the farthest northwest district. Under Solomon's rule, the tribes fell into near-permanent desuetude. The harsh rationalization of the quadrumvirate's and Solomon's power violated villagers' culture in both time and space.

Solomon sat near the heart of a vast web of eastern Mediterranean trade, which recovered its amplitude during the reigns of David and Solomon. The heart itself lay along the coast to the north, in the maritime cities of Dor, Acco, Tyre, Sidon, Byblos, and harbors farther north. Dor and Acco probably began under Solomon's rule. The Greeks called these societies Phoenician. The Israelites called them Canaanite (referring to their trade base) or Sidonian (referring to the mother city of the golden age of Phoenician culture in the tenth to eighth centuries, overshadowed by Tyre during most of the period).

Solomon received timber and gold from Tyre. One report put the gold, some of which came from Egypt, at five tons by the time Solomon had completed his and Yahweh's houses. In return, Solomon shipped to Tyre 100,000 bushels of wheat and one million gallons of olive oil each

4. On early Israel as a "tribal" society, see Niels Peter Lemche, *Early Israel: Anthropological and Historical Studies on the Israelite Society before the Monarchy* (Leiden: E. J. Brill, 1985), 67–69; Robert B. Coote, *Early Israel: A New Horizon* (Minneapolis: Fortress, 1990), chap. 4.

year, whether the rains came or not. This colossal quantity of food, added to the dedication feast and the thirteen years of work put in by villagers, was what the two houses, palace and temple, cost the people of Israel and Judah. Still it was not enough to pay off Tyre. Solomon turned over, in addition, twenty towns and villages in Galilee to its king, Hiram, who could afford to scoff at Solomon's generosity. It was all the same to the villagers, who became Phoenicians instead of Israelites and for whom, as for most villagers then, little more came with their name than a particular hierarchy of tax collectors. Over time conditions for villagers could change, but in ways not indicated by changes in names.

Wealth from many distant lands passed through Solomon's territories, brought by ship from west and south and by donkey and camel caravan from north and south. Solomon's alliance with Hiram gave him access to shipping on both the Mediterranean and Red seas. Phoenician cities had begun to trade again in the eastern Mediterranean in the eleventh century B.C.E.. Although there is no archaeological evidence for Phoenician settlement and colonization in the western Mediterranean until the ninth century, Phoenician pottery and metal artifacts from the eleventh century have turned up in not only Cyprus and Crete but also Sicily and Sardinia. The fleets under the corporate flag of Tyre and Jerusalem sailed to the far ports of Europe, Africa, and Asia. Either legend or annals put the figure for Solomon's annual income in gold at twenty-five tons. His palace wall was lined with two hundred large and three hundred small shields of pure gold. The ships brought in silver, ivory and ivory work, exotic animals, precious stones and woods, incense, spices, and linen and woolen garments. Transit through the Negeb was assisted by settlers there; the evidence is unclear whether they were garrisons under the direct command of Solomon or nomads allied to him, as they had been to David. Later in Solomon's reign, control of the Negeb route to the Red Sea was more difficult than earlier, since the kings of Egypt and Edom in concert harassed Solomon's forces out of the Negeb. Solomon was an arms importer and exporter. He got horses from Anatolia and chariots from Egypt, and he shipped horses to Egypt and chariots to Syria and Anatolia.

Solomon also initiated the export of the produce of Palestine, but in a less organized way than the kings of Israel and Judah less than a century later. In lieu of efficient state commodity export, many whole villages changed sovereign hands as Solomon's dominion gradually attenuated. Solomon kept his trade network intact through alliances sealed by diplomatic marriages and the practice of the cults of his trade partners. In Jerusalem and on the hills about the city, as well as around other major Israelite cities, alien merchants and trade groups pitched their huts, tents, and canopies and carried out the procedures of the cults of their own sovereigns, sanctioned by their trade partner Solomon, just as versions of Yahweh's royal cult were practiced in other capitals. These aliens came from Egypt, Moab, Ammon, Edom, Phoenician cities, Syrian cities, Hatti, Cyprus, possibly southern Arabia, and many more distant places. Most foreigners were respectfully impressed with Solomon's palace and temple. Few were overawed, since they often knew better at home.

COURT LITERATURE

According to the legend of the queen of Sheba's visit (an apparent anachronism as Sheba was a significant power only later), foreigners were expected to salute Solomon's literary attainments. The palace and temple scriptorium under his patronage kept busy not only with administrative records, diplomatic documents and correspondence, annals, catalogs, lists, and the training of scribal recruits but also with recording and revising lists of wise sayings—the prescriptive repository of courtly moderation, prudence, and fair-mindedness. This literature notoriously contradicted the consequences of king's rule in the experience of most of his subjects but served to confirm to the denizens of the court and their alien kind the propriety of luxury.

In addition, Solomon's scribes passed on slightly revised versions of documents from David's reign. They tied his apologetic compositions together with the official version of Solomon's birth and succession to produce the whole of what is now found in I Samuel 15 through I Kings 2. They modified the collection of David's prayers of the persecuted righteous man by adding to them many prayers and hymns of a different type. These included, for example, what is now Psalm 8, which acclaimed Yahweh as the creator of the monarchic priestly cult; Psalm 29, a hymn to Baal adopted, with merely a change of divine name, into the cult of Yahweh; and a new prayer at the beginning and end of the collection.

The prayers were performed by a choir and, judging from the theme of the Solomonic additions, became more declaration than petition. The opening song, Psalm 2, solemnly warned the kings on the fringes of Solomon's unraveling empire to kiss his feet (the text is doubtful, but the meaning is not) or else. The concluding song, Psalm 72, acclaimed Solomon's justice in clichés and solicited a continuance of the prosperity of his dominions (at least as evidenced by his own groaning board) and of blessings from the remaining vassals of his imperium. This last composition was assigned to Solomon, but a colophon indicated that

the entire collection had the authority of the dynastic founder David.[5]
Other psalms that now fall outside these bounds were also part of the
Solomonic temple service. These included the psalms extolling the
kingship of Yahweh over the nations, the psalm celebrating entrance of
the ark into the cult of the house of David (Psalm 132), and possibly
others.

Solomon's scribes left intact the J document, David's history of the
nation's purported nomad ancestors, with its emphasis on vassals'
endorsement of Yahweh's blessing. It was this last document that
Jeroboam I's scribe would get hold of and revise.

ISRAEL'S PHARAOH

The villagers of Palestine who saw Solomon's palace and temple or,
more often, heard about them were overawed, since such structures
surpassed everything in their immediate experience. Under Solomon,
social stratification in Israel worsened. The court recorders of
Solomon's peacespeak were unaware of the lives of villagers. Their
ignorance echoes in the words of the later court narrators of Solomon's
reign. The myriad workers, they serenely assumed, were as happy as
the king: "Judah and Israel were as many as the grains of sand at the
seashore; they ate, drank, and were merry." All were secure in the
peace signified by Solomon's name: "Judah and Israel held their prop-
erties in safety, each under their vine and fig tree, all the days of
Solomon."

The reality was otherwise. On average, villagers worked more and
ate less. They lived further below subsistence than in living memory
and begged more often for credit, with land and labor for security.
Their tribal patrons, having lost influence with the regime, suffered
their own hardship and were less in a position to help. Solomon's elite,
absentee proprietors of village land grants from the king, had little
history of social involvement with the villagers under their charge.

The collective cultivation rights gradually fell into the hands of
urbanites; the cultivators themselves served as tenants or debt slaves.
The policies of the quadrumvirate and Solomon brought the typical
monarchic social pattern to the Palestine highlands and locked it in
place for the rest of the biblical period. Social change was henceforth
variation on the theme of the extreme gap between the wealth of a few
and the poverty of the many, along with the breakdown of social relations across class lines. Any continuance of a tribal order in Judah was

5. The dating of Psalm 72 to Solomon requires that the references to Sheba in vv. 10 and 15
be considered interpolations, or that the entire psalm as we have it be a later composition
based on an earlier Solomonic composition.

thereafter a function of the influence of lords and fighters based in the desert margins of settlement, and of how dependent they in turn were on their ties to the house of David. In Israel the tribal order was largely replaced by a feudal order in which the monarchy was more· dependent on the landed fighters of the realm and hence the complex politics of highland area landowners.

The metaphor of the tribes of Israel as a concept for the nation lay embedded in the literature of David's court that set the standard for subsequent additions and revisions by later Jerusalemite scribes. The metaphor thus persisted in state propaganda long after the tribal relations in Israel between the thirteenth and early tenth centuries had disintegrated. This circumstance made an essential contribution to the preservation of the temple scriptures following the fall of the house of David, their patron state, and even of the temple itself one thousand years later.

David's state was a departure from the Israelite norm.[6] Solomon's overthrew the norm altogether. Israel as a political and social identity had stood for opposition to the city-based and chariot-backed harsh centralized rule of imperial lords preoccupied with trade in military and luxury goods and agricultural commodities and the paraphernalia of power and display. Solomon was a home-grown pharaoh, a son of Israel in name only.

POLITICAL DECAY

During Solomon's reign, Egyptian forces reappeared in Palestine. They were back in the fertile Philistine plain, prepared to treat with Solomon as they had two hundred years before with their vassal the historical Moses. The pharaoh held even Gezer, an important gateway to the hills of Jerusalem. He turned Gezer over to Solomon as a wedding gift when Solomon consented to an alliance by marrying one of his daughters. In Egypt's view, the alliance was only a prelude to forcing Solomon or his heir into vassalage to the mighty throne on the Nile.

Vassals to Solomon in outlying royalties found Aramaean and Egyptian support in defying him. Rezon, a vassal of Hadadezer of Rehob-Zobah, took a lesson from David and rebelled against his lord, gathered an outlaw band, and took over Damascus, where the city fathers recognized him as king. Solomon's ties to David's garrison in Damascus had degenerated like much else. Solomon lost all control over Rezon, and hence over the main road into Syria. Similarly, when David and Joab conducted a slaughter of men in Edom, a royal

6. See Coote, *Early Israel*, chap. 7.

scion named Hadad escaped through the Negeb and Sinai to Egypt. The pharaoh gave him an urban household, estates, and rations. He married a sister-in-law of pharaoh, and their son was raised in the royal palace. During Solomon's reign, Hadad went back to Edom and mutinied against the Davidic scourge in his land. The route to the south was jeopardized by his incursion.

By the end of his reign, Solomon was on the verge of losing Israel itself. One of his officers in Israel, ambitious to ride the crest of popular discontent to power, found harbor with the king of Egypt, along with other rebels against Solomon.

CHAPTER SIX

Jeroboam's Revolution

Tens of thousands of people in the heartland of Israel, the erstwhile kingdom of the house of Saul, despised Solomon's rule. Taxes had been crippling. Many villagers had been forced to put up their lands to cover debts and finally to give up their lands to pay them. In E, Jacob, who represents Israel, is a wage laborer whose wages had been changed capriciously and often, and the northern tribe of Issachar is named for the just wage he receives from God, not Solomon's men.[1] For debtors and the hungry with no land, debt slavery for children or self was the only alternative. When Solomon died, the villagers of Israel were determined to recover control over their lives and fortunes. Their stronger patrons, whose power had faded in the shade of Solomon's picked officers, henchmen, and mercenaries, were ready to lead the villages in a righteous cause. Egypt was eager to make its decisive contribution.

DIFFERENCES BETWEEN ISRAEL AND JUDAH

The central hills of highland Israel preserved quasi-tribal political forms and values in the face of Solomon's depredations, whereas Judah did not. This difference between Israel and Judah did not come about simply because Solomon was a son of Judah. It was one of a set of differences between Israel and Judah that had important consequences during the entire biblical period. Judah was a circumscribed plateau, bounded by steep foothills to the west and desert to the east and south. Only to the north did it merge with the hills of Benjamin. Rule in Jerusalem was often foreign, as in the Amarna period, and stable. The

---

1. For a treatment of the modern equivalent of responses open to the peasantry of Israel short of revolution, see James C. Scott, *Weapons of the Weak: Everyday Forms of Peasant Resistance* (New Haven: Yale University Press, 1985).

five-hundred-year rule of the house of David (approximately 1000
to 500 B.C.E.) was founded by a Judahite condottiere buttressed by
Aegean mercenaries, chief for a Negebite coup. David's origins in Bethlehem gave the regime local legitimacy, but its support came largely
from outside, sometimes far outside. Jerusalem's importance typically
extended far beyond its local region. David and his descendants did not
rule at the pleasure of the local big landowners or notables. In Jerusalem, the customary law of Judah was typically set aside in favor of
court law serving the development of distant ties. Solomon's flouting
of the law of sanctuary was symptomatic of the dual law of Judah: one
law for the city, another for the countryside.

The Israelite monarchy maintained its capital at or within a few
miles of the traditional center of the north-central highland, Shechem.
Although Israel was in some ways more porous than Judah to the outside world, the importance of its capital was limited to its own region.
This circumstance was again reflected in the Amarna period. The leading families of Shechem came from rural backgrounds or had close
connections with their rural clients. Close relations with the population of the region were essential, and rule depended on the support of
local notables. Families vied for rule more aggressively than around
Jerusalem, and one family could be overthrown by another, as happened nearly a dozen times in the short history of the kingdom of
Israel. Unlike in Judah, in Israel customary law normally applied in
the city as well as countryside. Departures from this norm were regarded with hostility throughout the society. The villagers of Israel
had a higher regard for their own patrons as fighters than in Judah.
Factional fighting usually swept through the whole of the northern
region, whereas in Judah it could be confined to a particular area and
hence more easily managed from the capital.[2]

These differences were based in part on geography. In comparison
with Judah, Israel was larger and received more rainfall, and therefore produced a larger agricultural and smaller pastoral product. It
supported a larger population that was politically more fragmented
among different geographical subregions. There were fewer natural
frontiers, practically no borders on agriculturally marginal lands,
and more openness to the plains and valleys of the region. The north's
comparative economic advantage in perennials was under the greater
control of local landowners, paramilitary nomads had less (though not

2. For the analogous circumstances in the nineteenth century, see Miriam Hoexter, "The
Role of the Qays and Yaman Factions in Local Political Divisions: Jabal Nablus Compared
with the Judean Hills in the First Half of the Nineteenth Century," *Asian and African
Studies* 9 (1973): 249–311.

negligible) influence, and defense and social order depended more on the region's landed magnates. These notables played a direct role as, alternately, supporters and opponents in the topsy-turvy politics of rule. Dynasties tended to be short-lived. During most reigns, interregional trade tended to be dominated by magnates. Low-cost transport by sea was more accessible. Goods traded in and out of Israel had a larger percentage of heavy items and fewer high-cost, low-weight luxuries than was the case in Judah. Expansion and intensification of agriculture took place primarily through the consolidation of land holdings and cash cropping. Such intensification also took place in Judah, but there the pastoral component was more significant. Israel was more immediately accessible to and from the main trade ways and hence of greater strategic importance to imperial powers. These comparisons did not always hold true, but they usually did.

Rulers in Israel were dependent on regional rural support and obliged to local custom. This gave greater scope not only to magnates but also to local holy men and women or saints in the north (usually called "prophets" in modern literature, following the Greek translation of Hebrew *nabi'*; Arabic *sheikh* or *wely*). These eccentrics functioned as power brokers among families, including strong families, and claimed, by virtue of their eccentricity, an uncommon connection with divine sources of power. This power expressed itself in various realms, including local cults, legal disputes over land tenure and debt, military ventures, sickness, and hunger. These people are seen in the political history of the north, again in a variety of arenas, more often than in the south. By the time of Solomon, Moses had been revered for generations in the north, and possibly Joshua as well. There were no comparable saints from the south (in part also because unlike the north, it was mostly unsettled until well into the eleventh century).[3]

The culture and politics of the north remained quasi-tribal in that the magnates as a class were able to preserve some, though far from all, of their power against the Davidic monarchy. It might not have seemed so at the peak of Solomon's power, but that did not last long. Rehoboam succeeded Solomon in Judah. His rule over Israel was no foregone conclusion. He would have to be confirmed in Israel by the magnates, and for this purpose he was obliged to journey to

---

3. See Robert B. Coote and Mary P. Coote, *Power, Politics, and the Making of the Bible: An Introduction* (Minneapolis: Fortress, 1990), 15 and *passim* (*s.v.* "Saints"); Robert B. Coote, *Early Israel: A New Horizon* (Minneapolis: Fortress, 1990), 26–27; Edward B. Reeves, *Hidden Government: Ritual, Clientalism, and Legitimation in Northern Egypt* (Salt Lake City: University of Utah Press, 1990); Scott D. Hill, "The Local Hero in Palestine in Comparative Perspective," in *Elijah and Elisha in Socioliterary Perspective*, ed. Robert B. Coote (Atlanta: Scholars Press, forthcoming).

Shechem and hear their complaints. The magnates of Israel, with Egypt's help, threw him out and authorized Jeroboam to fill the vacancy. The house of David thus was reduced to Judah. Except for a period under King Josiah, also with apparent Egyptian assistance, it would rarely include more.

JEROBOAM I

The magnates and villagers of Israel and the king of Egypt closed ranks long enough to carry through a revolution against the house of David. Together they approved the ambitious Jeroboam I to advance their causes. It is important to emphasize that the populace of Israel probably played a significant role in this revolution, partly on the basis of their real power and partly on the basis of their common identity stemming from the past of tribal Israel, a role not to be minimized despite the emphasis here on Jeroboam's role.[4]

Jeroboam had been Solomon's corvée officer for his home district, Ephraim. His father died when he was young, placing him in the class of the fatherless, and there is no reference to any brothers; thus, as was the case with David because of his comparative youth, Jeroboam's support within the family network was minimal. He became a fighter in Solomon's military, as David had in Saul's. In this service he may have sustained an injury later remembered as a paralyzed arm. When put in charge of forced labor in his district, which under Solomon included areas of both Ephraim and Manasseh, he was given sufficient power to enable Solomon to evade the established strongmen of the fractious territory of Joseph and yet still hold it. Jeroboam's urban base was Shechem, but as Solomon's man he depended little on its sponsorship.[5] Sometime during Solomon's reign, Jeroboam turned against his royal power source and rebelled against the tyrant in Jerusalem. The urban and mountain lords of the Shechem region, he reasoned, whose case against Solomon he adopted, would not remain within Jerusalem's sphere of power indefinitely.

4. For the history of this revolution, see J. Maxwell Miller and John H. Hayes, *A History of Ancient Israel and Judah* (Philadephia: Westminster, 1986), 218–49; J. Maxwell Miller, "Rehoboam's Cities of Defense and the Levitical City List," in *Archaeology and Biblical Interpretation: Essays in Memory of D. Glenn Rose*, ed. Leo G. Perdue, Lawrence E. Toombs, and Gary L. Johnson (Atlanta: John Knox, 1987), 273–86. The sources for our knowledge of Jeroboam I are meager in the extreme and completely inadequate for anything approaching history in the normal sense. Jeroboam existed, and there was a revolution. All else is inference, more or less. The historical problem is not so much whether a particular interpretation of the evidence is correct but whether the wider interpretative framework in which the evidence is placed makes historical sense. On the limits of a popular notion of tribal identity, see Coote, *Early Israel*, 75–83.

5. On Shechem in this period, see Robert G. Boling and Edward F. Campbell, Jr., "Jeroboam and Rehoboam at Shechem," in *Archaeology and Biblical Interpretation*, ed. Perdue, Toombs, and Johnson, 259–72.

Jeroboam did not build his power by playing family politics, since he did not have extensive family connections. His revolt against Rehoboam was like David's against Saul. He fished for support from disaffected strongmen and their bondsmen, and he welcomed the subornation of Israelites by Damascus and Egypt, the nodes of the northeast-southwest highway, as a counterweight to the Jerusalem-Tyre axis. Jeroboam's later placement of state cults in outlying towns and the movement of his capital to Tirzah, northeast of Shechem, confirm that his power did not rest with the bygone elites of Shechem. As an outlaw to the Davidic state, he took refuge with the Egyptians, as David had with the Philistines. Pharaoh Sheshonk (935 to 914 B.C.E.) gave him asylum, along with other Palestinian royal protégés rebelling against Solomon, until Solomon died. Jeroboam was from the western foothills of Ephraim, in the zone where Egyptian and Israelite territories merged. If he led a successful rebellion in Palestine, he could look forward to offering his retainers land in the Egyptian-held lowland, leaving the highland to the Israelite landed notables. In the volatile circumstances of the northern kingdom, however, whatever coalitions Jeroboam was able to piece together were unstable. E shows Jeroboam's anxiety in the face of this weakness; he scrambles to find support where he can, yet he still ends up doomed to insecurity.[6]

As mentioned, Egyptian power in the tenth century B.C.E. again snaked into Palestine, as it had during the New Kingdom. After Rameses VI (1142 to 1135 B.C.E.), the Egyptian pharaohs had not been much heard from for 150 years, during which time the Philistines ruled the southern coast. Then the pharaohs reappeared. David regarded Egypt as the ultimate threat to his rule. At the same time, Egyptian influence induced David and Solomon to organize their administrations on an Egyptian model. Solomon received Gezer from pharaoh and married a daughter of pharaoh. No previous instance of such a marriage with an alien is known. Some historians believe, therefore, that Solomon married not a daughter of pharaoh but a princess of the nobility. As others have pointed out, however, no kingdom as

---

6. For recent analysis of traditional and formulaic elements in the Deuteronomistic description of Jeroboam, see C. D. Evans, "Naram-Sin and Jeroboam: The Archetypal *Unheilsherrscher* in Mesopotamian and Biblical Historiography," in *Scripture in Context: 2. More Essays on the Comparative Method*, ed. W. Hallo, J. Moyer, and L. Perdue (Bloomington: Indiana University Press, 1983), 97–125; John Holder, "The Presuppositions, Accusations, and Threats of 1 Kings 14:1–18," *Journal of Biblical Literature* 107 (1988): 27–38. There is little about Jeroboam either in 1 Kings or hypothetically in E that does not compare with traditional beliefs about royalty and its complications. Nevertheless, there is no reason to doubt that some of what the Deuteronomist finds to report about Jeroboam was real. The overlap in the portraits of Jeroboam suggested by 1 Kings and E may indicate that the choice of traditional elements used to portray him was influenced by his real person.

powerful as the house of David had ever before arisen on Egypt's borders. The fortresses at Gezer, Beth-Horon, and Baalath were meant as bulwarks against Sheshonk, who in Solomon's time threatened to invade Palestine and in Rehoboam's carried out his threat. Sheshonk harbored troublemakers from Edom, Syria, and Israel, and in Rehoboam's fifth year campaigned in Palestine.

REVOLUTION

Jeroboam broke off the last big piece of the kingdom of the house of David outside of Judah. Jeroboam's revolution constituted not so much the division of the kingdoms, as it is often called, but the secession of Israel. It may be termed a revolution: not only did it overthrow the house of David but it also transformed social conditions in Israel by restoring the quasi-chiefdom that had existed there prior to the creation of the Davidic empire. The revolution crested on village unrest, magnate discontent, and Egyptian interference. Jeroboam found backing from five distinct groups: villagers, local saints, local landowners, parties of priests, and Egypt. Israelite magnates led their men to oppose the house of David, and Rehoboam's fortresses and chariots were of little use in putting down the rebellion. Jeroboam may also have had to embrace or subdue remnants of the house of Saul and Solomon's officialdom in Israel, but these gave him no lasting difficulty.

Solomon's death made the revolt easier by precipitating a struggle for the throne in Jerusalem, of which no notice is taken in the sources. The biblical texts leave unclear whether during the critical period of the revolt Jeroboam was still in Egypt or had returned to Palestine. Nevertheless, the events as described in preserved annals have a schematic veracity. Jeroboam had taken up residence with pharaoh along with other of Solomon's opponents. Safe in Egypt, Jeroboam could promise the Israelites relief from the state's corvée and shift the blame for harsh forced labor onto Adoram and Rehoboam, since he had been absent from his post as corvée administrator for some time. As Solomon's successor, Rehoboam came to Shechem to be acclaimed king of Israel. An assembly of Israelite magnates appealed on behalf of their clients to the crown to reduce its corvée requirement: "Lighten the yoke your father put upon us." As memory had it, Rehoboam brandished an obscene gesture and boasted that his phallus was fatter than his father's thighs. The yoke was to become a leaden burden and the whips, spiked rawhide.

The Israelites declared war. Young Rehoboam turned over the restoration of order to old Adoram, armed with decades of experience in quelling village worker revolts. The Israelite mob stoned Adoram to death in a communal rage fired by years of high-handed abuse. Rehoboam fled for Jerusalem. The battle line was drawn across Benjaminite territory, where it undulated for a generation. According to one tradition, Jeroboam was still in Egypt. If so, he had David's alibi, as well as his luck: he was somewhere else at the moment his onetime supervisor met his fate.

The sources say little about Jeroboam's primary supporters, Egypt and the Israelite landowners. The system of jurisdiction established by Jeroboam returned a measure of rule to the landowning strongmen of his realm and defined the urban and rural law as one, the norm for the region of Shechem. In the propaganda regarding his usurpation, the emphasis fell on popular backing. This is one of the few instances where the biblical texts describe a village revolt, although such revolts must have been common in biblical Palestine, as elsewhere. Popular support for Jeroboam was considerable. He restored the villagers' military; took steps to protect their legal rights; and thus used them not only to oppose the house of David but also to limit the power of their magnate patrons, on whom he was dependent. Nevertheless, as his adoption of J makes clear, once in power, Jeroboam was determined to replace his Egyptian godfather with local backers.[7]

JEROBOAM'S RULE

Ahiya (Ahijah), a saint of the venerable but wasted shrine of Shiloh and a likely protégé of the banished Abiathar, gave divine sanction to Jeroboam's appointment as king. Jeroboam, however, did not find himself obliged to restore the tribal shrine at Shiloh, and it is not mentioned in E. Following its destruction in the mid-eleventh century, Shiloh was resettled as a small village but never recovered its importance. (Nevertheless, according to royal annals, the same Ahiya condemned the house of Jeroboam to ruin, perhaps in response to Jeroboam's neglect of Shiloh.)

Bethel and Dan were also traditional tribal shrines, whose venerability ranked little lower than Shiloh's. There were priestly clans to accommodate. For these, the disused cults at Bethel and Dan were refurbished. The cults of Jeroboam resembled David's: local shrines supported local jurisdiction, and two border shrines hosted state compulsory pilgrimage cults, one at Dan near the border with Damascus

7. The sources provide no direct evidence for Jeroboam's relationship to Egypt following the revolution. Sheshonk campaigned through Jeroboam's territory five years later, apparently on more or less friendly terms, as Jeroboam was not replaced. E makes no elaboration or modification of the anti-Egyptian stance of J. There is little reason to speculate about Jeroboam's Egyptian policy, as it was probably complex and variable over the twenty-odd years of Jeroboam's rule.

and one at Bethel near the border with Judah and Jerusalem. There were city cults in both Shechem and Tirzah, but Jeroboam's primary state cult was separate from, and more prominent than, the cult of the royal capital. The affiliations and hostilities of the priestly houses in Jeroboam's time are the subject of inconclusive research. Jeroboam honored the settlement rights of the Davidic Levites but excluded them from service at the state cults. Some evidence suggests that a family of priests tracing their ancestry to Moses was paramount at Dan, in the region closer to Moses' historical bailiwick, and a family tracing to Aaron, a rival line of the Jerusalemite priests, at Bethel. To judge from the names of their founders, most, if not all, of these tribal priestly families claimed an Egyptian pedigree, a circumstance that fit conveniently with Egypt's early support for Jeroboam. The polemic in Exodus 32 against the establishment of a cult of a golden bull by Aaron probably came from the court of Rehoboam, if not from Hezekiah two hundred years later.

Jeroboam's state cult was his household cult, created at traditional sanctuaries on his own authority much like the cult of Micah described in Judges 17–18. Jeroboam revived the cult of the tribal warrior El, of which Yahweh was a manifestation, to reflect his military organization. El was conceived of as invisible, astride the traditional bull of El, the icon of his ancient epithet. These bulls contrasted with the stylized lions, or cherubim, of the shrine of the house of David. Lions symbolized war production and Jeroboam's bulls, the fair judgment of El and the agricultural production of the village, undermined by Solomon's outsized temple slaughter. The bulls of El further represented the deliverance from corvée slavery in Egypt celebrated in state lore from David's time, if not earlier, for the secessionist state of Israel owed its existence as well to delivery from corvée slavery. As indicated in E, one of the main rites of the cult was the unction of menhirs, or pouring olive oil on upright stones. The precise meaning of these menhirs is not known (see further in chapter 11). The emphasis on oil mirrored the importance of the main product of Israel at the time. Jeroboam probably put the brakes on the process of latifundialization, or commercializing consolidation of estates, for the production of oil that had been set in motion by Solomon. Fifty years later, under Omri and his successors, however, the state established by Jeroboam pushed that process to its extreme. Finally, Jeroboam apparently moved the cultic calendar later than in Jerusalem to accommodate the later harvests in the north.

Jeroboam did not dispense with forced labor any more than David had. He conducted building programs in Shechem, which had been shunned by the house of David, and in Penuel in the Jordan valley. These fortresses jeopardized the house of David's stronghold in Mahanaim and supported the shift in trade to the northeast promoted by Jeroboam. Jeroboam eventually seized Mahanaim. The main axis of the house of David had been northwest and southeast, as well as to Egypt. Jeroboam now predominated in the Egyptian trade. He shifted the axis for Israel's trade to the northeast, to Damascus, where during the time of David and Solomon a great kingdom was developing, holding off the Assyrians for two generations while the Levantine states continued to do battle with one another. Baasha, the chief from Issachar who overthrew the house of Jeroboam, had a treaty with Damascus, and Jeroboam probably did also.

Later in his reign, Jeroboam had Tirzah rebuilt and moved his capital there, a few miles northeast of Shechem and with direct access to the Jordan valley. Megiddo may have been closed to him through Egyptian control. Jeroboam moved to Tirzah when he felt strong enough to forgo whatever ties he may have formed with the main families of Shechem. The comparison with David's transfer from Hebron to Jerusalem is obvious. With a new capital and two state cults on his military borders, Jeroboam had shown himself able to stand with reduced magnate support. His main support, however, remained the families on Israel's borders, especially near the Egyptian zone. The E strand suggests an appeal to broad support, an indication that it was written early in Jeroboam's reign, about 930 to 925 B.C.E., in Shechem.

The house of Jeroboam failed to cultivate local support or control rival strongmen enough to last long after Jeroboam's death. His son Nadab was overthrown after a rule of only two years.

CHAPTER SEVEN
Adoption and Adaptation of J

Jeroboam I was a usurper with a measure of popularity. The coalition that launched him was broad. It was also shallow. As part of the effort to shore up his legitimacy, he had his court scribes write and revise documents in his favor. These writings have mostly disappeared. E may be the only one surviving. E was the revision of J carried out when Jeroboam appropriated J. That is, Jeroboam quite literally procured a copy of J—probably one that had lain for years in Shechem or Megiddo—and ordered it recopied with additions, thus stamping the history of Israel with his own seal.

A HOUSEHOLD REVISION

Jeroboam's additions to J dealt with his royal self, his household, and the cults that defined his household's jurisdiction, all of which were essential ingredients in the consolidation of power—and the same ingredients as J. The notion that E consists of various old sanctuary traditions of the populace of Israel is out of the question. E makes next to nothing of Jacob, who represents Israel, nor of Moses, the supposed folk hero of Israel. E is interested in Jacob solely as founder of the cults of Bethel and Gilead as E knows them, and in Moses as founder of the cult of Horeb. Conversely, E makes major additions to the story of Abram, the patriarch most closely associated with Judah and the house of David in contrast to Israel. However, E makes nothing of those few passages where Abram does have to do with Israel. His interest is attracted to Abram solely because in J, Abram founded the cults of Shechem and Bethel. Thus, E's concluding account of Abram, the near-sacrifice of Isaac, apparently takes place at Shechem.

Nearly every scene in E, from first to last, takes place in a royal court or court of law, including cult shrines and shrines-to-be as judicial centers. These scenes are viewed from the perspective of ruler or magistrates. The courts of law are sometimes informal, but E's focus remains the jurisdiction of the elite spelled out in detail in E's finale. Some of these scenes build on similar scenes in J, but E, unlike J, is virtually limited to such scenes. Of course, all groups in society had an interest in the law. But it was the ruler's responsibility, and prerogative, to sanction, certify, and regularize his law and jurisdiction, and it was to the carrying out of this responsibility that E made his chief contribution. In their role as agrarian clergy, Jeroboam's covey of scribes had no interest in transcribing the narrative traditions supposedly shared by Jeroboam's new subjects in order to give definition to some homogeneous culture of Israel. There was no such culture. Indeed, even if Jeroboam's scribes had wanted to create one, they would have had no way to publicize it and would in any case have been powerless to dissolve the cultural and political cell walls that isolated one family, clan, village, faction, and locality in Israel from another.

E's purpose was not to narrow the conceptual gap between ruler and people but to widen it, to promote not cultural homogeneity but the prerogatives of the new ruler and his henchmen. E contributed to Jeroboam's legitimacy by resonating not with the supposed traditions of the nation but with the ruling household, thereby consolidating the self-image of the regime. E was not a script to be broadcast from Radio Free Shechem to the village populace of Palestine but a mirror to be held up to Jeroboam and his court, albeit including villagers' patrons, for their satisfaction. When the king looked into this mirror, he saw little besides himself. Like J, E reflected, even if indirectly, mainly the life and concerns of its sponsoring monarch.

The events of the revolution itself, ironically, were already reflected in the base document J. Little, if any, change was required to turn J into a commentary on the reemergence of Israel out of bondage to the house of David.[1]

HISTORY BASED ON J

What was J? Shortly after establishing his rule in Jerusalem, David ordered a history of Israel written whose purpose was to appeal to the continued loyalty of the tribal sheikhs of the Negeb and Sinai who had contributed to his rise to power and frequented his court in Hebron, and who were now essential to the defense of his border with Egypt.

---

1. This apposite figure has occurred to many; see, for example, Baruch Halpern, "Levitic Participation in the Reform Cult of Jeroboam," *Journal of Biblical Literature* 95 (1976): 31.

This history was meant to suggest to them that they themselves represented the ancestral heads of David's nation—as they did, in the sense that early Israel was ruled by a circle of powerful tribal heads. According to J, which reflected more David's history than Israel's, the eponymous patriarchs of tribal Israel were Negeb nomadic sheikhs, not highland villagers. Israel was at peace with the Philistines. Tribes previously only loosely (if at all) tied to Israel, like Judah and Simeon, were made integral; indeed, the tribes of the south were among the eldest. The tribes tended to fight with one another but, by following the example of regal deference presented by Abram, were able to compose their differences. The antitribal cult of temples was condemned; only modest sacrifices on modest fieldstone altars were valid, even for the state. The most difficult agreement would be between Judah and the highland heart of Israel, represented by Joseph. Their conflict was resolved through the virtue of David's eponymous ancestor Judah.

The primal event of nation formation was escape from Egyptian corvée in the Delta, a harm more likely to overtake the Negeb pastoralist than the highland villager. The complaints and revolts against the kinglike rule of venerable Moses were numerous but illegitimate: such singular saviors from the snares of the evil empire—whether Moses or, by implication, David—were to be respected and obeyed absolutely. Any attempt to reverse the sacral legitimation of such rule and the blessings it brought, endorsed by vassal kings, would outrage none other than the divine creator, the god of David's state and, in J's presentation, David's "nation." This document, which historians call J, was retained by David's son Solomon and became the basis of the first four books of the Bible.[2]

Jeroboam became the king of most of an existing state and hence adopted the existing history of that state, just as Solomon had done. The clerics attached to his court and state cults had no problem with the house of David's cult history of the nation of Israel, and they read it to the king and his notable visitors to demonstrate his sympathy with his notables' hostility to the house of David. The comparison between pharaoh and Solomon was patent. The scribes of the state of Israel were likewise happy to take back the "official" history of the onetime tribes of Israel. Although Moses was a northern hero, Jeroboam's scribes added little to his story. They were interested in Joseph, who stood for Shechem and the heart of Israel, and their additions to his

2. For further detail, see Robert B. Coote and David Robert Ord, *The Bible's First History* (Philadelphia: Fortress, 1989).

story turned J's history of Judah and Joseph into the history of mainly Joseph.

The existing history was treated in two ways. First, J in itself was read as proof of the house of David's hypocrisy and injustice. E welcomed the chance to use the house of David's own words against them. Then, additions were made to J that reflected the house of Jeroboam's view of itself and the nature of its cults and jurisdiction. Thus, J was both adopted and adapted, and read in Shechem and Bethel. At the same time, it continued to be read in the rival court of Jerusalem. The contrast of interest is thus not between J and E but between J's J and E's J, or J and JE.

PUTTING J BACK ON ITS FEET

In J, the house of David delivered a propaganda bonanza into the hands of Jeroboam. Solomon's violation of David's claims of beneficence in J was so complete that anyone with access to J could well wonder why Solomon, who seemed to have destroyed everything David purportedly stood for, had not destroyed David's history of Israel as well. Solomon reversed the liberation from forced labor central to J. Jeroboam claimed to have liberated Israel from forced labor under Solomon. This was largely advertising on Jeroboam's part. He retained the corvée, as might be expected of a former corvée chief. The men his rereading was meant to impress benefited from corvée. It was their vassals, clients, and bondsmen and their families who suffered from it. J said nothing, furthermore, about other forms of labor exploitation. E exposes this omission by confirming the limitation of debt as state policy: E lays down the release of a debt slave after seven years of service.

Solomon's administration of Israel overrode and threatened to erase the traditional political identity of Israel's leaders, incorporated in J through the concept of the twelve tribes of Israel. Jeroboam restored tribal identity in theory. He did not, however, emphasize the tribes. Instead, he gave the authority of levy and jurisdiction to local strongmen regardless of tribal affiliation. The shrines mentioned in E are not based on tribal territories, and the number and organization of magistrates are not tribal. J, however, did illustrate at least the decentralized rule and jurisdiction inherited by David and violated by Solomon. E's emphasis on the multiplicity of Israel's cults underlines the perception that the temple represented a substantial departure from the decentralization allowed by J.

J portrayed the reconciliation of the tribes of Israel with Joseph, effected by Judah. In the person of Solomon, however, Judah treated the rest of Israel harshly. Jeroboam, in the role of Joseph, was prepared to be reconciled anew with all Israel except Judah, who had clearly discarded the trait of conciliation he possessed in J and therefore did not deserve consideration.

Solomon rejected any special relation between the north and Egypt, even though he himself may have entered into an extraordinary marriage alliance with Egypt. Jeroboam reaffirmed Joseph's "productive" relationship with Egypt, along with the relationship implied by Ephraim's and Manasseh's having an Egyptian mother. Indeed, according to one Greek tradition, Jeroboam, like Joseph, had an Egyptian wife. In J, the leader of Israel came out of Egypt, just like Jeroboam. Like Moses in E, Jeroboam lived at pharaoh's court, in pharaoh's favor. Jeroboam reincarnated both Joseph and Moses and as such had a greater claim than Solomon or Rehoboam to the narrative heritage of those great administrators and lawgivers. At the same time, the Egypt that tried to prevent Israel's liberation from forced labor, the cardinal point of J that Solomon flouted, was the enemy. In J, Moses killed the Egyptian taskmaster in just revenge for the hardship of forced labor, heralding the stoning of Adoram under essentially identical circumstances. J's Moses was a forced labor gang boss who turned and led his people in a successful revolt against state oppression. Having so many points in common with Joseph and Moses, Jeroboam could not have described himself better if he had written J himself.

In J, God opposed any cultic structure greater than a fieldstone altar. Solomon had a monumental palace and temple complex erected. The nature of Jeroboam's cultic construction is not certain, but it was probably much more modest than Solomon's and therefore closer to the intent of J than the house of David itself under Solomon. As for the god of the state cult, J's Yahweh was the tribal El only implicitly assimilated to the Davidic state. Under Solomon, Yahweh became indistinguishable from Baal. In their additions, Jeroboam's scribes made the restored character of El explicit by substituting for the name Yahweh the honorific *'elohim*. This was court advertising again: the distinction between Yahweh and El was not confirmed in the Israelite onomasticon (naming practices).

By appropriating J, Jeroboam maneuvered the house of David into scoring an own goal. Through his policies, Solomon had turned much of J on its head. Jeroboam was not going to let the house of David get away with it. He ordered his scribes to put J back on its feet and to drape it with a new garment, which historians call E.

CHAPTER EIGHT
Sons
in Danger

In agrarian Israel, the household was more than a family and its resources. It was the primary center of power. "It was the structure through which the magnate exercised authority; it was the vehicle through which he maintained inherited status; and in time of war or civil disturbance it was the instrument with which he defended himself or conducted hostilities. In short, it was an institution of the highest political and social importance."[1]

HEIRS TO RULE

The man whose revolution produced E was a man whose father died early enough that his mother was remembered as a widow (I Kgs 11:26). According to the annals, Jeroboam I's eldest son in Palestine suffered a mortal illness (I Kings 14). It is probable, moreover, that Jeroboam was required to surrender at least one son, and perhaps several, as a hostage to pharaoh's court in Egypt, as was the practice.[2] It is not known whether Jeroboam remained loyal to Egypt; his hostage son or sons were at serious risk at best, and at worst they could have been executed. To judge from this minute but consistent evidence, Jeroboam, whose meager household support was further weakened by a lost father and doubtful sons, was a man consumed with anxiety about fathers and sons. Such anxiety was common to his age. In his case it was compounded by circumstance.[3] For this reason, E depicts one incident

1. Nigel Saul, *Times* (London) *Literary Supplement*, 2–8 Sept. 1988, 969, in his review of Kate Mertes, *The English Noble Household, 1250–1600* (Oxford: Basil Blackwell, 1988).
2. See Othmar Keel, "Kanaanäische Sühneriten auf ägyptischen Tempelreliefs," *Vetus Testamentum* 25 (1975): 413–69.
3. The allusion to other sons of the house of Jeroboam in 1 Kgs 14:10–11; 15:29 belongs to a later stage of the assessment of Jeroboam; see John Holder, "The Presuppositions, Accusations, and Threats of 1 Kings 14:1–18," *Journal of Biblical Literature* 107 (1988): 27–38.

after another—from dangers to the sons of Abimelek to dangers to the son Moses—in which sons, and through them the father and mother, fall into grave jeopardy and survive by the slimmest of margins.[4]

E is also concerned with the position of mothers in the descent of property. J had acknowledged matrilineal descent in some instances, apparently reflecting David's concession to the strong families he married into in the tribal network of power. This principle would jeopardize Jeroboam's position as the channel of inheritance, in relation to his mother's brothers and even the ruling class of Egypt, through his possible marriage to an Egyptian. E therefore takes pains to neutralize J's instances of matrilineage with narratives stressing the prerogatives of the father.[5] Nothing less than the patrilineal dynastic inheritance was at stake, to which was added the restoration of traditional patterns of descent following the disarray brought on by Solomon. Because the king himself embodied the sacred, he regarded his inheritance as a sacred trust.

A monarch's ability to secure his rule as monarchic "property" depended in part on his ability to establish the succession of his heir. The monarchy was property to be passed on like any other, and one way to keep the property in the family and out of the hands of rivals was to demonstrate that there was a definite member of the family in line and ready to take over, and that the succession was under the protective oversight of the monarch's god. The monarch's concern for sons was the most visible example of a concern that extended throughout the society. Every family passed through this crisis. In this conception, the ruler's sons stood for the presumed highest public welfare in a complex network of family welfare.

ANCIENT PARALLELS

The concern for a royal heir finds expression in many ancient documents. In narratives delineating the foundation of state cults, the ruler-to-be typically defeats the forces of disorder, constructs his palace, and then fathers the royal heir. But the theme is more widespread than this. Of the three lengthy narrative texts preserved from the royal entrepôt of Ugarit on the Syrian coast, two begin with this theme.[6] These texts date to about three hundred years before E. In

---

4. Some historians have pointed to the similarity between the names of Aaron's two sons, Nadab and Abihu, who were reportedly killed by Yahweh when they offered "alien fire" (Lev 10:1–2), and Jeroboam's two sons, Nadab and Abiya. The story of the golden calf in Exodus 32 indicates that Aaron was connected in some way with the cult of Bethel. This similarity appears, however, to be a coincidence, as the names are of common types.
5. Nancy Jay, "Sacrifice, Descent and the Patriarchs," *Vetus Testamentum* 38 (1988): 52–70.
6. The translations that follow are from Michael David Coogan, *Stories from Ancient Canaan* (Philadelphia: Westminster, 1978), 32–35, 58–59, with slight changes.

one, named for the prince Aqhat, the legendary king Dan-El (or Danel), whose name means "El judges," had no son. Danel goes to the shrine of El to perform an incubation rite, in which he sleeps at the shrine, in this case for seven days, hoping for a favorable dream from El. El is called the "healer," since the lack of a son was thought of as a disability or illness. (This is a concept encountered early in E: "God 'healed' Abimelek and his wife and servants, and they bore sons.") The Ugaritic text is as follows:

> Then Danel, the Healer's man,
>> the Hero, the man of the god of Harnam,
> made an offering for the gods to eat,
>> made an offering for the holy ones to drink.
> Then he climbed onto his mat and lay down,
>> onto his pallet, where he spent the night.
> One day had ended, and on the second
> Danel made an offering to the gods,
>> an offering for the gods to eat,
>> an offering for the holy ones to drink.
> Three days had ended, and on the fourth
> Danel made an offering to the gods,
>> an offering for the gods to eat,
>> an offering for the holy ones to drink.
> Five days had ended, and on the sixth
> Danel made an offering to the gods,
>> an offering for the gods to eat,
>> an offering for the holy ones to drink.
> Danel climbed onto his mat,
>> he climbed onto his mat and lay down,
>> onto his pallet, where he spent the night.

Eventually Baal, the divine patron of monarchs, intercedes with El, the patron of fathers:

> Then, on the seventh day,
> Baal approached the gods' Assembly with his plea:
> "Danel, the Healer's man, is unhappy;
>> the Hero, the man of the god of Harman, sighs:
> he has no son, but his brothers do,
>> no heir, like his cousins;
> unlike his brothers, he has no son,
>> nor an heir, like his cousins.
> Yet he has made an offering for the gods to eat,
>> an offering for the holy ones to drink.
> So, my father, El the Bull, won't you bless him?
>> Creator of all, won't you show him your favor?
> Let him have a son in his house,
>> a descendant inside his palace."

El grants Danel's request and gives the order that Danel's wife will
have a son:

> She will become pregnant, she will give birth,
>   she will conceive;
> and there will be a son in his house,
>   an heir inside his palace.

Danel wakes up delighted:

> Danel's face was glad,
>   and above his brow shone.
> He opened his mouth and laughed,
>   put his feet on a stool,
>   raised his voice and shouted:
> "Now I can sit back and relax;
>   my heart inside me can relax;
> for a son will be born to me, like my brothers,
>   an heir, like my cousins.

Once his wife becomes pregnant, Danel returns to his royal duties.
The sequence—having a son and then restoring justice—is identical
to the overall sequence of E.

> Danel got up and sat at the entrance to the gate,
>   next to the granary on the threshing floor.
> He judged the cases of widows,
>   presided over the hearings of the fatherless.

In the other Ugaritic narrative that begins with this theme, King
Kirta is without son or wife. Like Danel, he performs an incubation rite
in search of a remedy. The comparison with Jeroboam is so startling
that it might be wondered whether the information we have about
Jeroboam is less historical and more based on traditional narratives.
Although this is probably not the case, the similarity does show that
Jeroboam's situation was not isolated. The text begins,

> Ruined was the house of the king
>   who once had seven brothers,
>   eight sons of one mother.
> Kirta our patriarch was destroyed,
>   Kirta's dynasty was finished.
> His legal wife went away,
>   his lawful spouse:
>   the woman he married left him.
> He had had descendants,
>   but one third died in childbirth,
>   one fourth of disease,

> one fifth Reshep gathered to himself,[7]
>   one sixth were lost at sea,
>   one seventh fell in battle.[8]
> Kirta saw his offspring,
>   he saw his offspring destroyed,
>   his royal house completely finished.
> His line was utterly ruined,
>   and he had no heir in his household.
> He entered his room and wept,
>   he repeated his words and shed tears;
> his tears poured
>   like shekels to the ground,
>   like fifth-shekels onto his bed.
> As he wept he fell asleep,
>   as he shed tears he had a dream;
> sleep overpowered him and he lay down,
>   but his dream made him restless.
> For in his dream El came down,
>   in his vision the Father of humanity.
> He approached and asked Kirta:
> "Why are you weeping, Kirta?
>   why does the gracious one,the lad of El, shed tears?
> Does he want to rule like the Bull, his father,
>   or to have power like the Father of humanity?"

After a short break in the text, Kirta is heard responding,

> "Why should I want silver and gleaming gold,
>   a controlling share in a mine,
> perpetual slaves, three horses,
>   a chariot from the stable, servants?
> Let me have sons,
>   let me produce descendants!"

El granted Kirta's wish.

BIBLICAL PARALLELS

Royal preoccupation with sons permeates biblical texts as well. In J, the birth of Isaac is the culmination of a treatment of this theme that dominates most of the first third of the narrative. In the account preserved in 2 Samuel 7, at the moment David became established in Jerusalem, the holy man Nathan approached him with the message from Yahweh that "You will not build *me* a house (temple), but I will

---

7. Reshep is the god of fever.
8. The mathematics are figurative.

build *you* a house (a son and heir, a dynasty)." The birth of Solomon became the determinative theme of the revision of a document from David's court that served as the primary legitimation of Solomon's dynastic succession.[9] A poetic observation imaginatively attributed to Solomon, Psalm 127, captures the point well:

> Unless Yahweh builds the "house,"
>   the ones who build it work in vain. . . .
> .   .   .   .
> Sons are a grant from Yahweh,
>   the fruit of the womb a reward.
> Like arrows in the hand of a warrior
>   are the sons of youth.
> Blessed is the man who has
>   a quiver full of them.
> He shall not be shamed
>   when they drive his enemies from the gate.

Likewise, the prophecies of Isaiah, which concentrate on the theme of the Davidic ruler in relation to the cult of the temple, repeat the theme of the birth of sons. They culminate in the proclamation that

> to us a child is given,
>   for us a son is born;
> rule will be upon his shoulder,
>   and his name shall be
> "The warrior El, father of booty, chief of justice,
>   counsels a marvelous event." (Isa 9:6)

The attempts of the rulers of Israel to establish a dynasty did not often stick. Jeroboam's son was overthrown after only two years, and his usurper's son suffered the same fate. Only with Omri's household, a half century after Jeroboam, did a dynasty last into the third generation. The event was extraordinary enough for Omri's state to be known for decades afterward as the "house of Omri." Struggling against the odds, Omri took the measure of elevating his son as co-regent during his own lifetime; to this son he gave the throne name *'ah-'ab* (Ahab), meaning "My father [Omri] is my brother [co-ruler]." During Omri's poverty-producing regime, many families in Israel suffered the loss of their sons or the fate of never having any, a calamity delineated in the folk narratives regarding Elijah and Elisha (1 Kgs 17:17–23; 2 Kgs 4:1–37; 6:24–31; 8:1–6).

---

9. P. Kyle McCarter, "'Plots, True or False': The Succession Narrative as Court Apologetic," *Interpretation* 35 (1981): 355–67.

JEROBOAM'S PROBLEMS

Given the importance of sons and the prevalence of anxiety about them, it comes as no surprise that Jeroboam, as a usurper, or thief, of Davidic property, should be so engaged with the welfare of his sons. Reference has already been made to the possibility that he lost sons as hostages in Egypt. The precedent for succession set by his predecessors in Israel and his contemporary in Judah was not encouraging. Jonathan failed to inherit from Saul, apparently the first king of Israel. Saul's son Eshbaal lost the kingdom after a rule of only a few years. Rehoboam failed to hold on to most of his inheritance.

The story of the death of Jeroboam's first heir, found in the court annals of Israel and revised by a later writer, takes place in Tirzah and thus comes later than the probable writing of E. Nevertheless, it epitomizes the king's concern.[10] Jeroboam's son Abiya became ill. Jeroboam sent his wife to the shrine at Shiloh, to Ahiya, the holy man who had pronounced his accession and could authorize the succession. Ahiya pronounced the death of Abiya, which occurred precisely at his mother's return home. A later writer at just this point added, in retrospect, that Ahiya also pronounced the fall of Jeroboam's house.

E's interest in child sacrifice, shown early in E, raises the question of whether Jeroboam was under pressure to sacrifice a son, either to coerce an attacker into lifting a siege or to safeguard the new construction of a city or shrine. A definite answer is not possible. It is also not possible to know whether under Jeroboam many other families in Israel, having borne the depredations of Solomon, faced the question of whether they would ever have viable families again.

This is the anxiety that animates E. It plays an important role in E because of its peculiar intensity for Jeroboam, for whom the reiterated restoration of security, often affirmed in favorable dreams, answers to the continual nightmare of ferocious cruelty that could at any time befall a chief of Israel and his family.

SONS IN E

The incidents in E of sons in grave jeopardy divide E into two parts. In the first part, much the longer of the two, these incidents are strung together in a continuous series of examples of sons whose lives are saved in the nick of time, highlighting the value of what E terms "houses" (Exod 1:21; New Revised Standard Version: "families"), meaning "sons." In the second part, such incidents cease in order to highlight

---

10. It could also mean that E was written late rather than early in Jeroboam's career, though I consider this less likely.

the establishment of the cult of Horeb and its vital law. The turning point is the revelation of God's name at Horeb, at the moment God determines to rescue *his* son (Israel) from imminent catastrophe.

Before Joseph

E opens with four incidents involving Abram. The first three are fashioned after elements drawn from J's history of Abram and Isaac. All four illustrate the dire jeopardy of sons. In quick succession God imperils and saves the sons of Abimelek and his men, Ishmael, and Isaac. E introduces his theme with a story composed of elements from J's accounts of pharaoh and Abram (Gen 12:10–20) and Abimelek and Isaac (Gen 26:6–11). In J, Abram and Isaac called their wife their sister, pharaoh took Saray, and Abimelek took Rebecca. Pharaoh learned of his error when he and his people were afflicted with plagues; Abimelek, when he caught sight of Isaac and Rebecca starting to make love.

E turns these elements into a story, the first of E's opening incidents, whose main point is Abimelek's risk and the jeopardy to his and his servants' ability to father sons. Abimelek's name, meaning "My father is king," echoes E's interest in the heir. Abram merely serves as foil to Abimelek and plays the role of Ahiya of Shiloh, the holy man to whom the jeopardized appeal. J's "plagues" are turned into the "death" of fathers and sons. When Abimelek takes Saray, God appears to him in a dream and announces, "You are dead." God, however, restrains Abimelek from abusing Saray and advises the fearful king to appeal to Abram to intercede and "keep you alive." If not, "you and everyone who belongs to you will be dead." God refers here not to their death but to their inability to have sons, as is made clear by the conclusion of the episode, "God healed Abimelek and his wife and servants, and they bore sons," and E's later use of "dead" and "alive."[11] The use of "heal" recalls the Ugaritic description of El the potent patriarchal "bull" as the "healer" of the king without a son.

The second incident is composed on the basis of J's account of Hagar's pride and distress in Genesis 16. In J, Saray forced the pregnant Hagar into the desert, where Yahweh's genie spotted her resting next to a spring and rescued her. E's version emphasizes the danger to the son of Hagar and Abram. E's God again directs the action from start to finish, quite in contrast to J. Hagar is driven into the desert with her son. She comes to no spring and soon runs out of water. The

---

11. The threat is the same as that to David, who was said to have lost his first son with Bathsheba because he was guilty of adultery and murder.

boy is doomed, so she abandons him beneath a shrub and distances herself to avoid having to watch his inevitable death. She wept, but "God heard the boy's voice," not her voice, as in J. God shows her a well, and she gives the boy water, in the nick of time.

E fashions the third incident on J's narrative of Isaac and Abimelek in Gen 26:12–33. The preceding mention of a well leads to the explanation of the name Beersheba, the "well of the oath (Swear-Well)." Beersheba lies in the territory of Simeon, whose jeopardy E features in his additions to Joseph's story. This is the jurisdiction in the southwest of Israel, lying between the heartland of Israel and Egyptian territory. When narrating the first of many episodes involving the cults of Israel, E stresses the oath that undergirds the peaceable adjudication of legal disputes, a primary function of the cults and the subject on which E concludes. The sanctity of the oath preserves peace not only in the present generation but with the "progeny and posterity" (Gen 21:23) that is of constant concern to E.

The fourth incident E composes with no prompting from J, to highlight the distinctive theme with glaring intensity. Appearing to Abram at night, presumably in a dream, God orders Abram to slaughter his son and incinerate him on an altar. The narrator explains that this is a test, but Abram may not know it. From the rest of E it is clear that God is testing Abram's obedience, or "fear"—the right disposition toward God's law, epitomized by the people's reaction at Horeb at the end of E—and Abram's trust that God will safeguard fathers, mothers, and sons in jeopardy. This incident concludes with the first act of cultic sacrifice in E. The combination of sacrifice, fear, and jurisdiction will be dealt with in greater detail in chapters 11 and 12. Abram, previously advised that "your long line of descendants shall be through Isaac," makes explicit his trust: "God will see to it there is a sheep, my son." Abram never expects to have to follow through and kill Isaac, but he is prepared to carry out God's order until instructed otherwise, and the awful pathos is scarcely relieved by Abram's exemplary compliance.

E makes the next insertion in J when Isaac's son Jacob first falls at risk. In flight from one household and far from the next, the endangered son stops at Bethel and, in a dream, sees the sovereign God intoning his guarantee to a fearful Jacob to "watch over you everywhere you go—I will not abandon you."

When the narrative reaches the birth of the northern mountain tribes, E replaces part of J's account with his own. Rachel, who with her slave Bilhah becomes the mother of the main tribes of Israel, is so far without sons and faces the same fate as Abimelek: "If you don't give me sons, I am dead." Jacob sees no way to thwart God: "Can I take God's place?" Rachel instructs him to produce children through her slave. The firstborn is Dan, the father of the territory of the other state cult of Jeroboam besides Bethel. Dan's name refers to God as the cults' supreme legislator and adjudicator. The next born is Naphtali, whose birth in E harmonizes with J's account of the birth of each son in a crisis or struggle. Finally, God relents and allows Rachel to bear a son. She gives Joseph a name that marks, as she might have said, God's saving her life: "God has gathered up my shame" from lack of sons of my own.[12]

In J, Laban responded to Jacob's tricks in kind, in an affable battle of wits. E earnestly weighs in on Jacob's side. To E, Laban is a simple cheat who is no better than the kulaks whose rank exploitation Solomon condoned, as well as an "Aramaean," a direct rival of the Israelites, and no Israelite himself. When Laban threatens to ruin Jacob, Jacob says, "God did not let him do me harm." In J, the wily Jacob devised his own rescue by breeding spotted sheep. E's addition makes God, again through a dream, the source of Jacob's rescue. Rachel and Leah suffer disinheritance, and with them Jacob's sons. It is time to escape with what they have and with the household teraphim, which apparently are tokens of their right to keep what they possess. Laban pursues them, with the power to destroy the lot. God warns him off. The incident reaches its characteristic crisis as Laban interrogates the escapees about the teraphim. "Anyone you find your gods with," Jacob hazardously protests, "will not live." As Laban rummages the tents, E's audience holds its breath through the horrific tension E has created by putting Rachel and Joseph in the direst jeopardy. The success of Rachel's ruse emboldens Jacob to challenge the legality of Laban's behavior item by item. Having exhausted their legal dispute, the two reach a settlement by the habitual cultic menhir.

In J, this crisis was repeated when Jacob met up with Esau. E is less interested this time, however, since Jeroboam's Israel had little direct dealing with Edom, which Esau represents. E, however, does inject his theme. Esau asks, perhaps in E's mind threateningly, about Jacob's sons. "These are the boys with which God favored me," Jacob responds and, repeating the point a moment later, thereby cautions Esau to keep his hands off.

---

12. E makes no additions to the naming of the four eldest sons, Reuben, Simeon, Levi, and Judah. The omission of Judah is as expected. Reuben and Simeon play significant roles elsewhere in E, especially in his favorite narrative section, the history of Joseph. Except as ancestor to Moses, Levi is missing from E altogether, an indication that E has no special interest in Levi, contrary to some recent treatments of E. Nor is E interested in Shiloh, likewise conspicuously absent. The passages adduced to show the anti-Aaronid stance of E do not, in my view, belong to E.

The sons of Israel complete their number with the birth of Rachel's younger son, Joseph's full brother, Benjamin. This is a close call, even in J, since Rachel dies in childbirth. E has the midwife reassure her: "Don't worry, this one is a son, too."

Joseph

J's history of Judah and Joseph, which E transforms into the story of Jeroboam's ancestor Joseph alone, gives E numerous opportunities to amplify the jeopardy of sons, starting with Joseph himself. Reuben displaces Judah as Joseph's first rescuer. E, however, changes the emphasis to Reuben's gamble that he could foil his brothers' plan if he could get Joseph into a pit, "hoping to save him and get him back to his father." Thus, in E, the eldest son takes the place of the father in caring for the jeopardized son. The brothers follow Reuben's advice. Reuben goes off, and when he comes back, he discovers that Joseph has been sold—some traders having happened by at just the wrong moment—bringing Joseph into greater danger than ever.

The traders sell Joseph to Potiphar, a name E abbreviates from the name of Joseph's father-in-law in J. E replaces J's brief explanation of how Joseph gets out of prison in Egypt with a lengthy account of Joseph's success in interpreting dreams. This account prolongs the crisis of Joseph's incarceration. Once Joseph becomes a ruler with a wife and two sons, he names his sons Manasseh and Ephraim for his release from "the trouble I had in my father's household," as well as for the good fortune that "God has made me fruitful in the land of my affliction." Both names are perfect emblems for the refugee Jeroboam, a son of Ephraim.

With Joseph established, E turns his attention to the jeopardy of the other sons of Jacob, Joseph's brothers.[13] We do not have to guess what E thinks the story of Joseph's brothers means. Joseph, who at one point bluntly announces, "I fear God," speaks for E when at the end he says to his brothers, who are afraid that Joseph is about to take revenge, "Don't worry. Can I take God's place? You devised evil against me, but God devised that it should be good, to achieve what he has done today, saving the lives of a great people" (that is, the lives of twelve sons and their sisters, wives, and potential offspring). This is a fair interpretation of J's story of Joseph as E found it. It remains for E to compound the sons' jeopardy and to highlight the providence of God.

---

13. E does not follow J in referring to Jacob as Israel after the birth of Benjamin, probably to avoid the implication that Judah belonged by nature to Israel. Of course, Judah was open to domination, as implied by Joseph's first dream.

The first, the jeopardy to sons, entails E's addition of the danger to
Simeon and the further dangers that stem therefrom. In J, all ten brothers who made the first journey to Egypt returned to Jacob; Joseph kept
no hostages. E has Joseph arrest Simeon, who is then virtually lost to his
father. "I fear God," Joseph blurts. "Let one of your brothers be incarcerated here, and the rest of you go." This order occasions a poignant
realization among the brothers: they showed no mercy to Joseph. E
plays up the contrast with Joseph's mercy: "We are at fault because of
the way we treated our brother. We saw his dire distress when he
begged mercy from us, but we refused. That's why this distress has
come upon us." Reuben muttered, "I told you so." Joseph listens and
then has Simeon taken into custody before their eyes. On their way
home, they discover they cannot rescue Simeon without putting themselves and Benjamin in the same jeopardy. E inserts their fearful reaction: "Trembling they said to one another, 'What is this God has done to
us?'" Back home, Jacob is devastated by the loss of Simeon. "You have
made me childless! Joseph is no more. Simeon is no more. And now you
want to take Benjamin away, too." Reuben, Jacob's eldest, proposes a
solution that introduces yet another jeopardy: "You may kill my two
sons if I do not bring Benjamin back to you." At this point in E's supplemented version of J, it is difficult to see how Simeon and Reuben's two
sons are going to get out of this alive, to say nothing of the brothers if
they go back to Egypt with Benjamin.[14]

E, however, expands on the saving device of the bribe. When the
steward takes his baksheesh, he attributes it to E's "God of your fathers" and restores Simeon to his brothers. Joseph sends the brothers
home a second time, along with Simeon and Benjamin. When the
concealed goblet is discovered along the way, however, they are sud-
denly in the most extreme jeopardy of the story. At this moment, when
they return to Joseph, E adds to their confession, "God has uncovered
your servants' wrongdoing." Joseph discloses his identity to them and
then hastens to reassure them: "It was for saving [your] lives that God
sent me ahead of you. God sent me ahead of you to provide you a
remnant in the land and to save your lives. It wasn't you who sent me
here, but God, in order to make me ruler over all Egypt." Jacob is
reunited with his son and grandsons at last and dies. The sons are

14. E accents the role of Reuben here and earlier not because he is "northern" but because
the jeopardy of his sons imperils the line of the firstborn, as confirmed by the jeopardy of
Simeon, the next born. See also Martin Noth's observation in *A History of Pentateuchal
Traditions*, trans. Bernhard W. Anderson (Englewood Cliffs, N.J.: Prentice-Hall, 1972
[German orig. 1948]), 230 n. 605. On the early significance of the tribe of Reuben reflected
in E, see Frank Moore Cross, "Reuben, First-born of Jacob," *Zeitschrift für die alttestamentliche Wissenschaft* 100 (1988): 46–65.

afraid Joseph will avenge his wrong on them, whereupon he reassures them definitively, as indicated above, that the point of the entire exercise, from Joseph's first dream to this moment, was to insure the survival of sons and their households in the face of extreme jeopardy. The result, E points out, is that Joseph survives to witness the birth of his grandsons and great-grandsons.

Moses

The last two examples of the theme of jeopardy are dramatically direct. J's "new king over Egypt" is a nasty king. J, of course, depicted the Israelites' jeopardy in terms of forced labor. E adds the danger to their sons. Pharaoh orders every newborn Israelite murdered. The midwives fear God, save the sons, and get away with making an excuse to pharaoh in characteristic E style: the Hebrew women are "alive." Because the midwives fear God, God gives the people of Israel more sons than ever in their harsh condition.

Pharaoh is not to be so easily crossed. He orders his court to assure that every newborn son of Israel be thrown into the Nile. A Levite gives birth to Moses and, when she can no longer hide him from the authorities, launches him into the Nile in her own fashion. An exposed infant, Moses has only hours to live. But none other than a daughter of pharaoh discovers him in time and, respecting some anonymous mother's ruse, hands him over to a wet nurse, who happens to be his mother. Thus, in quintessential E fashion, the infant son Moses survives critical danger and is adopted into pharaoh's household, to add to pharaoh's sons.

This last incident has reminded historians of the so-called legend of Sargon, ever since its publication in 1901:

> Sargon, the mighty king, king of Agade, am I.
> My mother was a [   ], my father I knew not.
> The brothers of my father loved the hills.
> My city is Azupiranu, situated on the banks of the
>   Euphrates.
> My mother conceived me, in secret she bore me.
> She set me in a basket of rushes, with bitumen she
>   sealed my lid.
> She cast me into the river, which rose not over me.
> The river bore me up and carried me to Akki, the
>   drawer of water.
> Akki, the drawer of water, lifted me out as he dipped
>   his ewer.
> Akki, the drawer of water, took me as his son and
>   reared me.

> Akki, the drawer of water, appointed me as his
>   gardner.
> While I was a gardner, Ishtar granted me her love,
> And for four years I exercised kingship.
> The people I ruled, I governed.[15]

Probably E again makes use of traditional lore in composing the novel tale of Moses' birth. The more striking comparison, however, is less with Moses than with Jeroboam himself.

E shows that as a person fears God and so displays the disposition proper to the judicial cults of God and Jeroboam, a son is saved. From Abimelek to the midwives, a dozen incidents of this type combine to assuage the fear of the man who authorized E that his sons might be lost and with them, himself.

---

15. James B. Pritchard, ed., *Ancient Near Eastern Texts Relating to the Old Testament* (Princeton: Princeton University Press, 1955), 119.

CHAPTER NINE

Joseph in E

Jeroboam, a son of Ephraim the son of Joseph, suffered grave peril at the hands of his "brother" Solomon and ended up in Egypt. There he enjoyed the privileges of pharaoh's court and was groomed as the ruler-to-be of most of Palestine, including Egypt's holdings in the lowland. J's figure of Joseph gave E the opportunity to prefigure Jeroboam, who, like his resourceful putative ancestor, owed his political survival to pharaoh and was launched into ruling orbit by pharaoh's decree. E's additions make Joseph the leading protagonist among the history's ancestral chiefs, producing the Joseph story as we know it (chapter 3). In comparison with Joseph, even Jacob and Moses, the ostensible heroes of Israel, receive little attention; in Moses' case, the attention is exclusively as a function of the cult of Horeb and its law.

The longest section of E narrative (only E's concluding itemization of laws is comparable in length) is the story of how Joseph gets out of slavery and prison by his wits and good judgment and, by channeling God's revelation, is promoted by pharaoh to assist with the administration of food that, in the midst of famine, will make it possible for his brothers and their households to survive. This is the subject of E's repeated epitome of the story of Joseph: the brothers meant evil, but God turned it into good for the brothers' sakes (Gen 45:7–8; 50:20).[1] Just as J reflected the circumstances of David's coming to power, E reflects the circumstances of Jeroboam's coming to power, through

---

1. Compare Sean E. McEvenue's summary of the first three E stories (by his count): (a) God intervenes with an instruction that sets up a horrific situation, (b) Abram obeys, (c) dangerous consequences ensue, and (d) God intervenes to bring good out of evil; "The Elohist at Work," *Zeitschrift für die alttestamentliche Wissenschaft* 96 (1984): 317. Although in E, God brings good out of evil, the dangerous situation does not always derive from God's instruction.

Egypt. Joseph, in Jeroboam's likeness, is God's favorite, through whom God's providence is fulfilled. The history of Joseph is enhanced to stress God's providence in the revival of the tribes of Joseph under Egyptian auspices.

The pivotal event, Joseph's successful interpretation of the prisoners' and pharaoh's dreams—by far the longest single episode in E— leads to the rise of an exiled Palestinian in a foreign land with a boost not from his family but from a foreign king who, like Abimelek of Gerar, with Joseph "fears God." The comparison with Jeroboam at just this point is so strong that in addition to being the longest episode in E, it is the only one to take the place of a section of J apparently thrown out altogether.

Joseph is the triumphant denizen of the court. Joseph's wisdom is akin to Solomon's; E's explication of it in allusion to Jeroboam serves the same purpose as the story of Solomon at the beginning of his reign in which he asks God for wisdom and effective judgment and then, by solving the case of two prostitutes and their infants, demonstrates that God has granted his request (1 Kings 3). Joseph's wisdom and good sense mirror Jeroboam's similar pretension of enlightened rule.

Jeroboam's policies and even personal experience are represented in the E additions to J. Take Joseph's dreams. Jeroboam can be his own interpreter of dreams and oracles, if necessary, and may not have to wait on the likes of Abram and Ahiya.[2] "The interpretation of dreams belongs to God" and those who have direct access to God. Eleven stars bow to Joseph. One of the stars is Simeon, situated on the way to the Israelite cults of Beersheba and Horeb in the Sinai. Even Judah is one of the stars—a sign that Jeroboam would, like any monarch, enjoy conquering Judah if he could, and that he expected to win his war against Rehoboam. The most important elements in the first dream, however, are the questions, "Are you planning to be king over us? Are you planning to rule us?" These are the questions that the chiefs and magnates of Israel are asking Jeroboam after they have finally just thrown off the yoke of Rehoboam. What gives you, Jeroboam, or anyone, the right to assume the royal prerogatives we have just torn out of the hands of the house of David?

The point of E's story of Joseph as a whole is to answer this question on Jeroboam's behalf. The answer is clear: you may not like it ("They hated him all the more," "You devised evil against me"), but God did it ("God devised that the same should be good"), and it turns out to save

---

2. Whether or not Jeroboam himself was an interpreter of dreams, this motif augments E's emphasis on incubation.

your lives ("to save the lives of a great people")—so you had better like it.

E adds that the man who bought Joseph was pharaoh's captain of the bodyguard, in order to lay the basis for his lengthy account of the (God-given) court dreams and Joseph's interpretation of them. The cupbearer's and baker's dreams concern pharaoh's power to assign a person to an office or remove him from it. This is the power pharaoh held over Jeroboam, a mere foreign opportunist with hope for a placement in Palestine, whose son pharaoh could hold hostage.

Out of J's account of the seven-year famine, E fashions his story of pharaoh's dreams and Joseph's interpretations. Joseph concludes, "Let pharaoh look for a wise and discerning man to place in charge." Pharaoh is as alert to the acts of God as was Abimelek: "Has there ever been a man like this, with the spirit of God in him? After God has informed you about the famine and the plans for famine relief, no one can match you for wisdom and discernment." Joseph and Jeroboam get the job—of bringing the tribes of Israel back to life.

When the brothers arrive searching for food, "Joseph remembered the dreams he had dreamed about them," the link between the beginning and end of E's Joseph story. Joseph decides to test his brothers the way God tests people.

In J, all ten brothers depart for home. E, however, does not pass up this opportunity to introduce the issue of hostages that lay close to Jeroboam's heart. In E, Joseph takes Simeon hostage, presumably like Jeroboam's son. By now the brothers themselves recognize the work of God: "Now we are being made to pay for [Joseph's] blood. . . . What is this God has done to us . . . ? God has uncovered your servants' wrongdoing."

The brothers return with Benjamin. Joseph blesses Benjamin, not because he is Joseph's full brother (a reason appropriate to J) but in order to seal the superiority of Joseph over Benjamin (Jeroboam's tribe over Saul's) as Jeroboam takes over what had been, prior to David and Solomon, territory belonging to the house of Saul.

When Joseph discloses himself, he declares with finality, "God sent me ahead . . . . God sent me ahead . . . . It wasn't you who sent me here, but God . . . . God has made me lord over all Egypt." By implication, there can be no doubt that such a God has the sovereignty to make Jeroboam lord over all Israel. "Are you planning to rule as king over us?" the sons of Israel ask Joseph. No, Joseph says in effect, *God* is planning to *make me* rule as king over you.

The pharaoh who promoted Joseph is pleased, E emphasizes, when told that Joseph's brothers have come and that the siblings have been

peaceably reunited. This dispels any worry—or wish—in Israel that
the king of Egypt prefers to foster dissension, to divide and rule.

On his way to Egypt, Jacob makes a stop at Beersheba, the shrine
founded by Abram and confirmed (in J) by Isaac, in the territory of
Simeon, the son whose life was directly saved by developments and
who thus stood for the whole family. Joseph's wider family arrives en
masse to live off Egypt. J stressed their continuing work as herders,
whom the Egyptians abhorred. E stresses the rest and security that at
last come to Jacob in Egypt, after an arduous lifetime of journeying:
"I have spent a hundred and thirty meager and awful years wandering
here and there." Now Jacob "blessed pharaoh," a greeting and parting
formula that, however, frames his gratitude to pharaoh for granting
to him and his sons pensions from the income of valuable estates
in Egypt.

In time, Jacob falls ill and approaches death. Into J's story of Israel's
blessing of Joseph's sons Manasseh and Ephraim, E inserts the text
of the blessing. Because in J, Joseph himself was already heartily
blessed, E's blessing compounds the good fortune bestowed on the
tribes of Joseph. In E, Jacob prays that Joseph or his family will eventually return to Palestine.

E's final addition reiterates his theme that this is not the brothers'
evil but God's good, and he mentions Joseph's long life and his blessing
of his great-grandchildren. E concludes with Joseph's request to have
his bones brought to Palestine when his family returns there. as Jacob
wished. Further on, E mentions that "Moses took Joseph's bones
with him—Joseph had made the Israelites swear when he said, 'When
God without fail attends you, bring up my bones from here with
you.'" Joseph's bones became the relics that resanctified the shrine of
Shechem founded by Jacob and alluded to in the near-sacrifice of Isaac,
at Moriah. For centuries, and during at least the beginning of Jeroboam's reign, Shechem was the political center of highland Israel.[3]

E's Joseph story is not a general expansion of J's narrative of the
ancestor of E's court patron Jeroboam. E's enhancements are designed
to bring out or elaborate features in J's narrative that mirror Jeroboam's
rise as a protégé of pharaoh and as God's instrument for saving the lives
of Israel's tribes from the ravages of the house of David. Joseph is
Jeroboam, and Joseph's shrine, Jeroboam's first capital. It is to E's story
of the shrines of Israel and their rites that we now turn.

---

3. The stress on the patriarchal *wely* (saint) bones of Joseph might also have contributed to
Jeroboam's sense of the support of the *wely* Joshua and his burial shrine for his cause; see
chap. 13, n. 12.

CHAPTER TEN
State Cult and Country Shrines

The main subject of the third part of E (chapter 4) is the shrine of Horeb: its founding, rites, and laws. This part begins with two episodes relating to the birth of the founder of the shrine, Moses. The rest of E relates to Horeb itself.

Horeb is the last of a series of shrines described in E. The others appear in the first part of E, entwined with the stories of dangers to sons. J made little of the cults of Palestine other than Sinai. Noah's altar was left unlocated. Abram's altars at Shechem, Bethel, and Hebron and Isaac's at Beersheba established David's claim over the territories of these centers. However, J merely mentioned the altars at these sites, stressed their modesty, and referred to no other altars. Penuel and Sinai were the only other shrines mentioned. In contrast, E refers to additional sites and several times describes the menhir and rites of unction and incubation that characterized the Israelite cults he knew.

CULTS AND JURISDICTIONS

Jeroboam I depended on local landowners and strongmen in the olive-growing areas of Palestine to support him. The territories controlled by such strongmen had attached to them various cults, which were the centers of the jurisdictions held by local strongmen in their role as magistrates. In addition to the state god in Palestine, there existed supernatural forces on this earth in the form of local transcendent powers and persons specially related to them. In Jeroboam's Israel, the state could not ignore these altogether but had to accommodate them in some way. These were the spirits, ghosts, demons, genies, and sprites of trees, hills, rivers, and villages. They were joined by the forces of mana, stars and planets, the evil eye, magic, superstition, witchcraft, signs, and wonders. "What is often described as the natural tendency of Semitic religion towards ethical monotheism is in the main nothing more than a consequence of the alliance of religion with monarchy."[1] Villagers knew the gods and goddesses of all Palestine—El, Baal, Athtar, Athtart, Anat, Asherah, Dagon, Reshep, Shamsh, Horon, and others—because they influenced production and reproduction as much as spirits and magicians did.

However, these deities represented one kind of mysterious force among many, and they had to compete for the villagers' attention with local forces that might have a much more direct and immediate influence in home, field, or well. The villagers had nothing to do with the gods as the lords knew them, with the rational specification of the work of the various gods, the theory of their behavior and influence, the prescribed prayer service of their official cults, and the study of scripture—all activities sponsored by the cults of the elites. For the villager, the world of gods and spirits was the world of the village: the unchanging care for work, the gains and losses of production, the alternating dignity and shame of social contact, the scarcely relieved hardship of illness and debt, the capricious favoritism, the fatalistic complaining and manipulation—whatever pertained to the life of work.[2]

The teraphim stolen by Rachel were figurines used in household cults of gods and ancestors (there being little difference between these). Possession of them marked the right of descent of property, as well as household health and well-being. Along with the ephod, they were also used in shrines for divination, especially necromancy. E accepts the use of such figurines; when Jacob buries them by the shrine of Shechem, he apparently means to exclude them only from the state cult of Bethel.[3]

To what extent local magistrates exercised direct control over the cults of their district shrines is not known and may have varied. The norm, however, was for the cult to provide the prime sanction of local custom and of the strongman's form of justice, as well as to provide the

1. W. Robertson Smith, *The Religion of the Semites: The Fundamental Institutions* (1889; reprint, New York: Schocken, 1972), 74. On the sites of the many country cults of Israel, see Aug. Freiherr von Gall, *Altisraelitische Kultstätten* (Giessen: Töpelmann, 1898). On the piety of such cults, see preliminarily Hermann Vorländer, "Aspects of Popular Religion in the Old Testament," in *Popular Religion*, ed. Norbert Greinacher and Norbert Mette (Edinburgh: T. & T. Clark, 1986), 63–70; P. Kyle McCarter, Jr., "Aspects of the Religion of the Israelite Monarchy: Biblical and Epigraphic Data," in *Ancient Israelite Religion*, ed. Patrick D. Miller et al. (Philadelphia: Fortress, 1987), 137–55. Many older works of scholarship were attuned to this dimension of Palestinian piety in the biblical era.
2. Robert B. Coote, *Early Israel: A New Horizon* (Minneapolis: Fortress, 1990), 27–28.
3. See H. Rouillard and J. Tropper, "*TRPYM*, rituels de guérison et culte des ancetres d'après 1 Samuel XIX 11–17 et les textes parallèles d'Assur et de Nuzi," *Vetus Testamentum* 37 (1987): 340–61; Nancy Jay, "Sacrifice, Descent and the Patriarchs," *Vetus Testamentum* 38 (1988): 65–66; Karl van der Toorn, "The Nature of the Biblical Teraphim in the Light of the Cuneiform Evidence," *Catholic Biblical Quarterly* 52 (1990): 203–22.

site where the judicial claims of the weaker should, in theory, have received a fair hearing. The household as a political organism at the level of territorial magistracy was encouraged to eat and worship together to develop a common identity embodied in their patron, and to increase their political effectiveness. The territorial cult played a key role.

What was true for the local magnate was equally true for the man who aspired to royal power. Jeroboam's first purpose was to draw together the many households in his patronage, whose backing he required, in the distinctive cult of his state. The locations of Jeroboam's state cult were the border pilgrimage shrines of Bethel and Dan. However, E does not even mention Dan as a shrine, only as a son born and named, and he acknowledges many other shrines. Jeroboam thus supported the country shrines of his magistracy as well, with their associated holy men and priests, as he strove for both political coherence and uniform justice in his realm.[4] For E, the cults bear mainly legal interest, as legitimating the inherited jurisdictions of local notables so rudely infringed by Solomon.

HOREB

Horeb holds pride of place among the shrines mentioned in E. Bethel achieves a near second. E culminates at J's Sinai, which E renames Horeb, "Waste, Desert." For J, Sinai meant the southern Sinai, the site of the main military border cult of David. By Solomon's time, when "Israel" no longer controlled the Sinai, Sinai stood metaphorically for Zion, the site of the novel cult of Solomon's dynastic temple. Jeroboam's border cult was at Bethel, and he had no temple cult like Solomon's. Horeb, E's substitute for Sinai, was one way of dissociating Israel's cult from Jerusalem. Symbolically, Horeb continued to refer to the Sinai, now well out of the house of David's sphere of influence. At times during the period of the monarchy, Israelites may have made a pilgrimage to the Sinai. Whether this was possible in Jeroboam's time is not known. In practice, Horeb alluded to Bethel, the successor to Shiloh (also at this time "wasted") and the Israelite answer to the unprecedented, baneful cult of Jerusalem.

The importance of Horeb to E is underscored by the shrine's place in E's periodization of history. J divided history into three epochs of seven generations each and understood his own generation to mark the beginning of a fourth epoch. E's conception of epochs is different.

4. E's relative lack of interest in the priests and priestly clans in attendance at the country shrines reflects Jeroboam's concession to their multiplicity, decentralization, and probable weakness.

Like J, he uses the revelation of God's name Yahweh to distinguish the basic epoch. God reveals his name Yahweh when Moses discovers the shrine at Horeb. There are, however, only two periods in E: before the discovery of Horeb and the name of God, and after. Although in J the epochs of history were associated with the cultic naming of Yahweh, they are defined by generations. In contrast, the two epochs in E depend entirely on the revelation of the cultic name, which bisects E's additions to the story of Moses. The cults, headed by Horeb and its law, are fundamental. As in J, in E the cult is the basic legitimizing institution.[5]

E'S SHRINES

The shrines of E in order of appearance are as follows:

Beersheba

Beersheba apparently remained within Israel's jurisdiction during much of the period of the Israelite monarchy. It is mentioned in the story of Elijah and in Amos as an Israelite shrine. Beersheba lay on the supposed pilgrimage route to Horeb. In E's additions, Jacob made a stop to sleep at this shrine on his way to Egypt to rejoin Joseph.[6] Israel's (rather than the earlier house of David's) control of the shrines of both Dan and Beersheba was probably the source of the formula "from Dan to Beersheba."

Moriah/Shechem

E refers to the "Land of Moriah," which for him means the "Land of Fear." In J, Abram erected his first altar near the terebinth of Moreh at Shechem. E refers to this terebinth in his second episode involving the Shechem cult. Probably E has fashioned his name of the shrine of Shechem after J's name for the terebinth, just as he made up the name of Joseph's master from a name in J. "Moriah" alludes to the cultic "fear," or reverence, of concern to E. Not surprisingly, Shechem, Jeroboam's first capital and the object of his first building campaign, is mentioned twice more in E's story. The shrine of Shechem mentioned later is perhaps to be distinguished from Moriah, though the latter must have been nearby. Jacob erects a menhir in a

---

5. Previous literature on E seems to overstate the supposed struggle in E against religious apostasy and syncretism. This is apparently due to placing E in the same context as the stories of Elijah and Elisha, or with other "prophets" of the ninth or eighth centuries B.C.E. The assignment of Exodus 32 to E has also contributed to this perception.
6. It is surprising that E did not begin the cultic additions to J with Abram's erection of altars at Shechem and Bethel. Apparently, the cult of Beersheba took precedence. Whether this was due to E's relation to Egypt, his concept of Simeon's jeopardy, or some other factor is unclear.

field he bought outside of Shechem, and it is here that Joseph's bones are to reside.

Bethel

Bethel is the "house, or shrine, of El" (*beth-el*) of most interest to E after Horeb. It was the site of Jeroboam's southern pilgrimage cult, on the border with his main political rival, Rehoboam.[7] The cultic themes of E concentrate in E's additions to the founding of the cult of Bethel. The menhir is mentioned for the first time: it was Jacob's headrest as he slept, and every other menhir must borrow from this association. Jacob sleeps and dreams, and he hears God say, "I am with you." On waking, Jacob fears, or is awed, because the place is "fearsome." He erects the menhir and anoints it with oil, and he then vows a tenth of his production to the shrine.

For E, Bethel is a model shrine. In E's additions to the story of Jacob and his sons, God orders Jacob to lead his household in pilgrimage from Shechem to Bethel. All participants are to turn over their god and goddess figurines and earrings to be buried beneath the terebinth of Shechem's shrine, presumably for safekeeping, one of the important functions of any country shrine. As the pilgrimage progresses, the fear of God keeps the people of the towns and villages along the way from molesting Jacob's troop. They arrive at Bethel and erect a second menhir, with the name El-of-Bethel, the God who appeared to Jacob the first time he was there.

Gilead

The shrine at Dan is not mentioned by E, which lends all the more weight to Bethel. The menhir shrine in Gilead, described in E's addition to J's story of the stone pile commemorating the treaty between Laban and Jacob, takes Dan's place as a marker of the military border with Damascus.

Mahanaim

Mahanaim was an Israelite and Davidic stronghold in Gilead that fell into Jeroboam's hands during the revolution. E's reference makes clear that it is named for the same genie messengers that Jacob saw in his dream at Bethel. Between the "genies of God" and the bands of holy men who sometimes congregated at country shrines there would have been little difference in appearance.

7. Bethel is made the key to the interpretation of E by Hans Klein, "Ort und Zeit des Elohisten," *Evangelische Theologie* 37 (1977): 247–60. Klein makes the interesting, but unlikely, proposal that E was originally a guidebook to the shrine at Bethel, written by a sort of Israelite Pausanias.

[Penuel]

J told a story about Jacob's wrestling with one of God's genies at Penuel. According to annals available to the Deuteronomistic historian, Jeroboam ordered new construction at Penuel, an established Israelite shrine (1 Kgs 12:25). Whether written before or after such construction, E should have been interested in Penuel and have been expected to make an addition at this point. Two circumstances stopped him. Jacob's behavior did not express his concept of cultic dread, and J had already made the incident one involving "God" instead of Yahweh, to serve as an explanation of Penu-*el*, the "Face of *God*." Thus, no changes were necessary for this incident to be taken as E-like, if not the same as E.

Weeping Oak

The shrine of Weeping Oak was somewhere south of Bethel, even closer than Bethel to the border with Judah. A holy woman named Deborah was venerated there. It is possible that some confusion arose with the holy woman Deborah mentioned in Judges, whose palm, where she sat in judgment, was located "between Ramah and Bethel" (Judg 4:5); such a mix-up would introduce an explicit reference to jurisdiction at this shrine. For E, Deborah is Rebecca's wet nurse. This oak, not far from Bethel, receives the treatment of E's prototype shrine: "Jacob erected a menhir at the shrine and poured out a libation on it and poured oil upon it."

Rachel's Tomb

J located Rachel's tomb near Bethlehem, an unlikely location for the shrine of the mother of Joseph and Benjamin except for a pro-Davidic writer like J. E's addition suggests that this shrine was indeed in Israel's territory, not Judah's; it was on the way to Bethlehem, as J expressed it, but not in, or even necessarily near, Bethlehem.

Horeb

As explained, in Jeroboam's time the epithet Horeb alluded to the lengthy desert pilgrimage trek to the Sinai, and to the condition of the disused shrine of Shiloh. As the paradigm for cultic jurisdiction, it referred to Bethel. J's narrative of Moses at Sinai concentrated on Moses' discovery of the shrine, where Yahweh told Moses he would organize "Israel's" escape from Egypt, and on the rules of "Israel's" cults of sacrifice. J began with Moses' seeing the bush burning. Here E inserts his revelation and etymology of God's name. "I will be with

you," says God, using the verbal expression *'ehyeh 'immak.* Moses asks
for a name. "The proof is this: when you have brought Israel out of
Egypt, you shall all serve God at this mountain." God goes on, "I will
be *['ehyeh]* what I will be *['ehyeh].*" This tautology refers to what
God has just said: "I will be *with you.*" God proposes a name based on
the repeated "I will be": "Tell them I-Will-Be sent you." Then, with a
slight change, God turns this expression *('ehyeh)* into God's usual
name in Israel: "Tell them Yahweh *[yahweh]* sent you." Thus, E expresses the regime's reluctance to make much of the divine name mis-
used, in their judgment, by the house of David. At the same time, E
gives the name a distinctively Elohist interpretation: Yahweh means
"God will be with you," the essential dictum of comfort, providence,
and security made in the cults of Jeroboam.

JUDICIAL MAGISTRACY

In J, all this occurred while Moses was residing with his father-in-law.
When Moses and the Israelites approached this area later, after fleeing
Egypt, Moses' father-in-law came out to greet them. Moses explained
recent events to him and received his blessing, the culmination of the
episode for J. Then the Israelites proceeded to Sinai. For E, this is the
beginning of the episode anticipated by God's words, "You shall serve
God at this mountain"—in all, the grand finale of E. E disregards J's
itinerary and places Moses' encounter with Jethro at Horeb, as shown
by the insertion of "at the mountain of God" prior to J's "Israel came
to the desert of Sinai." Here E explains how the centrally controlled,
but still decentralized, judicial magistracy of Jeroboam's reign was
first organized by Moses, following Jethro's advice. This is followed
by Israel's enactment of the rite of approaching God for judgment,
the fearsome manifestation of God, and the laws to be adhered to by
the magistracy. All these unfold at Horeb, and all are what is meant in
E by "serve God" and "fear God." The cultic service of the trying, but
providential, God Yahweh lies at the heart of prescribed judicial piety
in the realm of Jeroboam. And, to repeat, it occupies the whole of the
third part of E.

The shrines lie along a Damascus-to-Egypt route that bypassed
Dan. Jeroboam's realm was open to invasion and outside influence
from all directions, but the focus of his attention was on the Damascus-
to-Egypt axis, as explained in chapter 6. Hence the shrines mentioned
by E lie in all directions except northwest, where the threat was least.
These were the directions where the support of local strongmen had
the greatest strategic effect.

CHAPTER ELEVEN
Revolutionary Spirituality

Certain elements of ritual and spirituality, or piety, in the age of Jeroboam I stand out in E's descriptions of the rites of the shrines. Some of these elements have already been referred to, but it will be helpful to explain them in order. The state and country cults were fulcrums for the main concerns of E: all the principal issues addressed by E are amplified in those cults.

EL

The god of Jeroboam's cults was El. State cults in E's time typically expressed the elite preoccupation with armed coercion; conquest; defense; and the administration of food collection, storage, and disposition. Baal was the typical divine guardian of the city-state and subject of such cults. Baal engaged in armed struggle, vanquished his opponent, built his palace (temple), fathered his sons, insured the productivity of the land, and maintained and defended the established orders of society. He was a favorite of king and producer alike. Solomon's Yahweh was indistinguishable from Baal. El, in contrast, was the tribal chief of chiefs in Palestine. He dwelt in a tent like a warrior; in the highland, desert, or by the sea, coastal or subterranean (typically thought of as montane); on the paths of trade and communication the tribes typically plied; and far from such paths, where the tribes typically took refuge. As "father of humanity," El was the guarantor of prodigious procreation, the male genius of household reproduction, as we have seen. El contributed most to the character of Israelite Yahweh, whose name probably was an epithet of El.[1]

---

1. Historically speaking, the name Yahweh is the verbal portion of a fuller name or epithet in the form of a statement: *yahweh-el*, "El [or less likely, the god] causes to be." Frank M. Cross has argued that what El caused to be was the military hosts of the divine warrior:

Although El appeared as Yahweh in Israel, at the same time El clearly retained a distinctive identity of his own. Jeroboam made much of El's distinctive character to evade Solomon's nefarious perversion of "Yahweh" and to pay respect to the "tribal" identities of his Israelite subjects. El manifested himself in distinct forms at particular shrines. Thus, the God of Beersheba is named El; the God of Bethel, El-of-Bethel; and the God of Shechem, El-Is-the-God-of-Israel. In lists of shrine deities kept in palace bureaucracies, such distinct Els were sometimes referred to simply as El number 1, El number 2, and so on. E makes more of the Els of the different cults than that. The plural form of El found in E's term *ʾelohim,* "God," is an honorific conveying the awe appropriate to God's manifestation.

In E, El's most characteristic pronouncement is "I am with you," which recurs repeatedly.[2] Behind this phrase lies the assurance that God provides water, food, and clothing to those who contribute a tenth of their production to the shrine, as Jacob did. The phrase also signifies the security gained through the revolution against the house of David and its cult, as the country shrines are revived and newly legitimated.

MENHIRS WITH OIL

The service of El at many cults involved contributing agricultural fruits—as vowed by Jacob—usually for the support of the local priesthood or holy men or women. The most characteristic cult object in E,

---

Canaanite Myth and Hebrew Epic (Cambridge: Harvard University Press, 1973), 60–75; cf. J. J. M. Roberts, "El," in *Interpreter's Dictionary of the Bible,* supp. vol., ed. Keith Crim, (Nashville: Abingdon, 1976), 255–58. As observed by Cross himself (p. 63), however, the attested examples of such a name refer to the birth of a child: "El has brought a child into being" or "May El bring a child into being." See Herbert B. Huffmon, "Yahweh and Mari," in *Near Eastern Studies in Honor of William Foxwell Albright,* ed. Hans Goedicke (Baltimore: Johns Hopkins University Press, 1971), 283–89. A derivation from childbirth places the name Yahweh at the focal point of El's concern for reproduction.

Again, the birth of sons on the one hand and political, or military, strength on the other are not separate. This is given striking expression, with reference to El, in Isa 9:4–6, which describes the birth of a scion in this way: "The yoke of the nation's forced labor, the bar for its shoulder, and the slave driver's cudgel he has smashed as on the day of Midian. Every boot treading in tumult and garment rolled in blood became fuel for the fire. For a child has been born for us, a son given to us. Just judgment is on his shoulder, and the name of this son is 'El the warrior, the patron with booty, the commander of justice, gives marvelous counsel.'"

The objections to this derivation of Yahweh made by Tryggve N. D. Mettinger (*In Search of God: The Meaning and Message of the Everlasting Names* [Philadelphia: Fortress, 1988], 31–33) are of interest, though his alternative proposal is not convincing. Other possible alternative etymologies of Yahweh include "(El or the god) blows (as the storm wind)," as proposed by Ernst Axel Knauf (*Midian: Untersuchungen zur Geschichte Palästinas und Nordarabiens am Ende des 2. Jahrtausends v. Chr.* [Wiesbaden: Otto Harrassowitz, 1988], 45) and "(El or the god) pounces (on booty or plunder)."

2. Gen 20:22; 28:15, 20; 31:3, 5, 42; 41:38, 39; 48:21; Exod 3:12; in addition to many instances in the third person.

however, is the menhir.[3] Jacob erected a menhir at Bethel and poured olive oil on it to mark his meeting with his ancestral El. He erected a second menhir in Gilead to mark the boundary between Aramaean and Israelite spheres of control. He erected a third menhir again at Bethel, on his return from Aram, and a fourth by an oak near Bethel to mark Deborah's tomb site, which he likewise anointed with oil.

Such standing stones were common and had a number of uses. One historian distinguishes four: memorial, legal, commemorative, and cultic.[4] The menhirs in E combine all of these uses. The purpose of most menhirs, as E conceives them, is to memorialize the dead, or heroes departed, in a cultic context where the application of law takes place. Moreover, the menhirs receiving the greatest attention in E mark Israel's borders with Judah and Damascus, and hence the territory to be bequeathed to Jeroboam's son. We can further explore what E means by his emphasis on the menhir by looking again at one of the Ugaritic texts illustrating a ruler's desire to have a son, as well as at some biblical texts.

Recall that since Danel ("El-*judges*") had no son, he went to the shrine of El to sleep and pray. There he made sacrifices of food and drink to the gods for seven days, until finally his plea was heard. Danel's prayer was for "a son in his house, a descendant in his palace." In lines not previously quoted, Danel's plea went on:

> To set up a menhir for his divine ancestor,[5]
> a family shrine in the sanctuary;
> to free his spirit from the earth,
> guard his footsteps from the Slime;

3. On menhirs, dreams, child sacrifice, and teraphim, as well as other apparent cult elements not considered here, see further the information collected in Karl Jaroš, *Die Stellung des Elohisten zur kanaanäischen Religion*, 2d ed. (Göttingen: Vandenhoeck & Ruprecht, 1982). Like many interpreters, Jaroš believes E was written in the late ninth or early eighth century B.C.E. (after Elijah and Elisha, and before Hosea) to address religious integrity and syncretism. He thus accepts the designation of Syro-Palestinian cult practices as "Canaanite," which cannot help but suggest an opposition with "Israelite" and a situation of *contrasting* cultures and ethnic *mixing*. This (perhaps unintentional) perspective, whose tenacity testifies to the magnetism of Deuteronomistic rhetoric, has lost much of its validity over the last twenty years because of numerous studies showing that "Israel" was and remained "Canaanite"; see Michael David Coogan, "Canaanite Origins and Lineage: Reflections on the Religion of Ancient Israel," in *Ancient Israelite Religion: Essays in Honor of Frank Moore Cross*, ed. Patrick D. Miller, Jr., Paul D. Hanson, and S. Dean McBride (Philadelphia: Fortress, 1987), 115–24; Robert B. Coote, *Early Israel: A New Horizon* (Minneapolis: Fortress, 1990), esp. 177 n. 5.

4. Carl F. Graesser, "Standing Stones in Ancient Palestine," *Biblical Archaeologist* 35 (1972): 34–63. On the current state of archaeological evidence for menhirs in biblical Palestine, see John S. Holladay, Jr., "Religion in Israel and Judah under the Monarchy: An Explicitly Archaeological Approach," in *Ancient Israelite Religion*, ed. Miller, Hanson, and McBride, 249–99; Neil Asher Silberman, "Standing Stones: *Masseboth* and Stelae," *Biblical Archaeology Review* 15, no. 2 (1989): 58–59.

5. In other words, his father's ghost. Or possibly: "for the god of his father," like the same phrase used in E when Jacob erects a menhir to mark his agreement with Laban.

to crush those who rebel against him,
    drive off his oppressors;
to hold his hand when he is drunk,
    support him when he is full of wine;
to eat his offering in the house of Baal,
    his portion in the house of El.[6]

The references to menhirs in the Old Testament outside of E fall into two groups. In the majority of references, menhirs are found in the context of altars and sacrifice, signifying the meal shared with gods and departed ancestors alike.[7] In the second group, the menhir commemorates the "name" of a man, with or without heirs. David's son Absalom, for example, erected a menhir with the thought "I have no son to commemorate my name," and he gave the menhir the name "Monument of Absalom."

These Ugaritic and biblical references make clear that E's emphasis on menhirs stems from the same set of beliefs and behavior as his emphasis on the jeopardy of sons. Jeroboam fosters the cult of the menhir, with its accompanying communal sacrifice, its "offering in the house of Baal, portion in the house of El," to memorialize departed family heroes in numerous local shrines, including possibly his own father. At the same time, against the backdrop of anxiety regarding his own attenuated household, Jeroboam longs to have an heir who will do the same for him, not to speak of the other services mentioned by Danel, including driving his enemies from the gate. Jeroboam supports the cultic services of magistrate families throughout his realm as one more component of his appeal to his cohorts and followers. Like herms in Greece, menhirs also marked the cults of local worthies, or heroes—living, like Ahiya of Shiloh, or bound to their tombs (also *wely* in Arabic)—who could be called on for advice, endorsement, or assistance by local strongmen about to take action.[8] In describing how Joseph's sheaf "set itself up" in the midst of his brothers' prostrate sheaves, E uses a term exactly like menhir to confirm the authority of Jeroboam (Joseph) despite his endorsement of the decentralization of jurisdiction.

---

6. Coogan, *Stories from Ancient Canaan* (Philadelphia: Westminster, 1978), 33, slightly altered.
7. Examples include Exod 24:4; Deut 7:5; 12:3; 16:21–22; Hos 3:4; 10:1–2; Isa 19:19.
8. See chap. 6 n. 3; Duncan Fishwick, *The Imperial Cult in the Latin West*, vol. 1,1 (Leiden: E. J. Brill, 1987) 3–5; Theodore J. Lewis, *Cults of the Dead in Ancient Israel and Ugarit* (Atlanta: Scholars Press, 1989). E is also interested in the cult altars on which sacrifices are prepared. These, however, were prescribed in J and need no further attention from E. J made no mention of menhirs; this is where E's additions concentrate.

The service of the menhir in E features unction, or pouring olive oil on the stone—the commonest product on the commonest element of the landscape. The service of Deborah's shrine also includes libation, probably of wine, and this practice may tacitly apply to the other menhirs as well. Anointing with olive oil may symbolize the feeding and care of the departed, not unlike anointing the corpse with oil. The production of oil in Israel expanded during Solomon's reign. Although the production and export of oil caused great hardship on Israel's villagers, Jeroboam did not want to reverse this economic development. The chief beneficiaries were the local strongmen who controlled the cults fostered by E. E's particular focus may suggest the promotion of cults of increased oil production.[9]

Archaeologists have discovered socles for menhirs in the temple fortress of Shechem built about 1150 B.C.E. These very standing stones may have been known to Jeroboam. Menhirs were common in the cults of Palestine, but it is noteworthy that the menhirs of the temple cult of Jeroboam's first capital, from the period just prior to the revolution, were prominent enough to produce monumental remains.

ALTAR SLAUGHTER

An essential ingredient of the ritual reflected in E is altar sacrifice. In Hebrew, *sacrifice* meant simply the slaughter of an animal for consumption, by gods, humans, or both. This "sacrifice" constituted the shared meal that reinforced the identity of the extended household essential to social position and political action.[10] Meat was an uncommon item in the average diet of biblical Palestine. People generally ate meat only at sacrifices accompanying a particular festival or commemoration. *Altar* (Hebrew: place or means of slaughter) and *menhir* appear side by side in numerous biblical passages. The relationship between

9. See William G. Dever, "The Contribution of Archaeology to the Study of Canaanite and Early Israelite Religion," in *Ancient Israelite Religion*, ed. Miller, Hanson, and McBride, 233: "A further reflection of the agricultural basis of this new society and religion is the recent evidence for production of olive oil in the immediate vicinity of several of these Israelite shrines."

10. Nancy Jay, "Sacrifice, Descent and the Patriarchs," *Vetus Testamentum* 38 (1988): 52–70, points out that sacrifice is essential to social order defined according to the link between father and son in many societies, not just Israel: "Ancestral sacrifice defines patrilineage boundaries ritually by distinguishing between those who have rights to participate and those who do not. Ancestor cults are not simply 'worship' of the dead; they are ways of organizing relations among the living." J appears to condone matrilineage. In Jay's analysis, E rectifies this threat to patriliny by resolving lines of descent that are ambiguous in J and by referring often to sacrifice as confirming patriliny. Jay's insight into sacrifice is valid even if she understates the incidence of sacrifice in J and overstates it in E. Jay's analysis supports the likelihood that Solomon's policies undermined patrilineal bonds and that Jeroboam's strengthened them.

sacrifice and the erection of menhirs is suggested by Exod 24:4, though it is not an E text: "After recording all Yahweh's words, Moses arose first thing in the morning and constructed an altar at the foot of the mountain and twelve menhirs for the twelve tribes of Israel."

Both concluding scenes in E, which take place at the shrine Horeb, involve communal meals of sacrifice. When Jethro comes to meet Moses in the desert, he "took a whole burnt offering and other sacrifices for God, and all the sheikhs of Israel gathered to eat food with the father-in-law of Moses in the presence of God." After Jethro advises Moses on judicial procedure, God manifests himself in a fearsome storm and pronounces the laws of Jeroboam's realm. Then, in E's last scene, Moses and the magistrates of Israel ascend Horeb and eat and drink in view of God. Although Moses goes up still higher, it is as though these cardinal magistrates are privileged to ascend halfway up the palatial stairway seen by Jacob at Bethel, to the throne of God.

NO CHILD SACRIFICE

One particular form of sacrifice is invalidated by E—the sacrifice of son or daughter. In the world of the Bible, this appalling custom was indeed practiced, by the people of Palestine and elsewhere, though many may have regarded it as little less repulsive than we do. Child sacrifice is not only a savage rite but also appears to contradict the purpose of sacrifice in the cult of ancestors and offspring stressed by E: to confirm and strengthen household bonds. E addresses this contradiction by placing Abram's near-sacrifice of Isaac early in his additions and making it the most wrenching instance of jeopardy to a son in the entire strand.

Child sacrifice was performed in crises of defense, like withstanding a siege or constructing a stronger wall or gate. One of the earliest references may come from a Ugaritic text, again about three hundred years before E:

> If an enemy force attacks your city gates,
>   An aggressor your walls,
> You shall lift up your eyes to Baal and pray:
> "O Baal,
> Drive away the enemy from our gates,
>   The aggressor from our walls.
> We shall sacrifice a bull to you, O Baal,
>   A votive pledge we shall fulfill, namely
> A firstborn, Baal, we sacrifice,
>   A child we shall fulfill,
>   A tenth of our wealth we shall tithe to you,

> To the temple of Baal we shall go up,
> In the footpaths of the house of Baal we shall walk."
> Then shall Baal hearken to your prayers,
> He shall drive the enemy from your gates,
> The aggressor from your walls.[11]

Exactly such an occurrence is described in 2 Kgs 3:25–27. The Moabite capital was under siege. "When the king of Moab saw that he was losing the battle, he took with him seven hundred swordsmen in an attempt to breach the enemy lines. When this failed, he took his firstborn son, who was to succeed him as king, and incinerated him as a whole burnt offering on the city wall." A great anger came on the besiegers, and they decamped.[12] According to an annal in 1 Kgs 16:34, only decades later than E, a warlord of Bethel refortified Jericho; to insure the foundation of its walls, he sacrificed his firstborn son, and to insure its gates, his youngest son. One purpose of child sacrifice was to insure the integrity of fortifications and defense, one of the prime reasons for having sons in the first place.

As an inducement for child sacrifice, however, public crisis and security were more exceptions than the rule. Tens of thousands of children were sacrificed in the Phoenician colony of Carthage during some six hundred years; their remains constitute the largest cemetery of sacrificed humans known.[13] Hundreds of urns containing the ashes of burned children have been excavated; these are interspersed with urns containing the remains of lambs and kids, occasionally sacrificed in place of a child, exactly as in E.[14] Terminology distinguished between sacrifices of elite offspring and commoner offspring. Sacrifices by the elite were far out of proportion to their numbers. The commonest reason for sacrifice was the fulfillment of a vow. Classical sources indicate that these sacrifices were to Kronos, or Saturn,

11. Translation derived from Baruch Margalit, "Why King Mesha of Moab Sacrificed His Oldest Son," *Biblical Archaeology Review* 12, no. 6 (1986): 62–63. See also A. Herdner, "Nouveaux textes alphabetiques de Ras Shamra," *Ugaritica VII* (Paris: 1978), 31–8, and "Une prière à Baal des ugaritains en danger," *Proceeding of the French Academy of Inscriptions and Belles Lettres* (CRAIBL) 1972, 694. See the critical comments on Margalit's understanding of this text by Jack M. Sasson in *Biblical Archaeology Review* 13, no. 2 (1987): 60; the correctness of Margalit's translation hinges on the wider evidence for child sacrifice, which Sasson views with much skepticism.
12. The anger is usually taken to be the wrath of the city's guardian deity. Margalit takes it to be the psychological trauma of aversion that affected the attackers. See the critical comments of Sasson in *Biblical Archaeology Review*, 12–15, 60, and of Bradley Aaronson in *Biblical Archaeology Review* 16, no. 3 (1990): 62, 67.
13. See Lawrence E. Stager and Samuel R. Wolff, "Child Sacrifice at Carthage—Religious Rite or Population Control?" *Biblical Archaeology Review* 10, no. 1 (1984): 30–51.
14. In Carthage in the seventh century B.C.E., one-third of the sacrifices were animals. Later, in the fourth century B.C.E., the ratio had dropped to one in ten.

corresponding to the Phoenician and Palestinian El, the patron of childbearing.[15] A menhir was often erected to memorialize the child. In Palestine, child sacrifice was performed not only in Jerusalem (2 Kgs 16:3) but also at country shrines (Isa 57:1–10).[16] Normally, the firstborn was selected for sacrifice, but not always. Some evidence at Carthage suggests that ritual infanticide was used in part to regulate the population, as infanticide has almost universally functioned (in preference to abortion).[17] More generally, the ritual of infanticide was a means of condoning the necessity of infanticide. Among the elite, it may have played a minor role in the consolidation of family wealth by limiting the number of heirs.[18]

It is clear that E's account of El's ordering Abram to sacrifice Isaac was not a situation made up out of whole cloth. E describes a situation that occurred in the households of the strongmen of his realm and the mitigation that also occurred, the substitution of a sheep. Both situation and mitigation were rooted in precedent. E's aversion to threats to offspring extends to discouraging, if not outlawing, child sacrifice.[19] Jeroboam himself may have been under social compulsion to sacrifice his son during a siege or for the refortification of Shechem or Penuel. E's notion of social and political security provided by El suggests a need to compensate for the malicious cruelty spurred by Solomon.

PILGRIMAGE

The pilgrimage cult entailing an installation in, and pilgrimage to, a military border zone, a perennial feature of Palestinian spirituality,

---

15. Compare the remarks from the Phoenician historian Sanchuniathon that "at the occurrence of a fatal plague, Kronos immolated his only son to his father Ouranos, and circumcised himself, forcing the allies who were with him to do the same," and that "when war's gravest dangers gripped the land, Kronos dressed his son in royal attire, prepared an altar and sacrificed him"; Harold W. Attridge and Robert A. Oden, Jr., *Philo of Byblos, The Phoenician History: Introduction, Critical Text, Translation, Notes* (Washington, D.C.: The Catholic Biblical Association of America, 1981), 57, 63. The coincidence that Shechem and his kin were forced to circumcise themselves, in the only such scene preserved in the Bible (Genesis 34), lends support to the supposition that Moriah was in E in the vicinity of Shechem.
16. See also 2 Kgs 17:16–17; 23:10; Jer 7:30–32; Mic 6:6.
17. Abortion was physically traumatic and dangerous. It also prevented choosing the sex of the victim. Although most references in texts are to the sacrifice of sons, it is likely that daughters were in fact more often the victims.
18. On child sacrifice, see further A. R. W. Green, *The Role of Human Sacrifice in the Ancient Near East* (Cambridge: American Schools of Oriental Research, 1976); Jo Ann Hackett, "Religious Traditions in Israelite Transjordan: Child Sacrifice," in *Ancient Israelite Religion*, ed. Miller, Hanson, and McBride, 131–33; Mordechai Cogan and Hayim Tadmor, *2 Kings* (New York: Doubleday, 1988), 266–67; Mark S. Smith, *The Early History of God: Yahweh and the Other Deities in Ancient Israel* (San Francisco: Harper & Row, 1990), 132–38; Shelby Brown, *Late Carthaginian Child Sacrifice and Sacrificial Monuments in Their Mediterranean Context* (Sheffield: Sheffield Academic Press, 1990); Patrick Tierney, *The Highest Altar: The Story of Human Sacrifice* (New York: Viking, 1990). For Genesis 22, see Philip R. Davies and Bruce D. Chilton, "The Aqedah: A Revised Tradition History," *Catholic Biblical Quarterly* 40 (1978): 514–46.
19. To repeat, it is not E's point to oppose a "foreign" cult practice with an "Israelite" solution.

played a significant role in upholding Jeroboam's revolution. The main pilgrimage cult described by J was that of Sinai, which E translated into Horeb and treated as a paradigm for cult jurisdiction. For E, the important pilgrimages themselves were to Bethel and Dan, Jeroboam's answers to the cults of Jerusalem and Damascus. We have already seen, however, that whereas E makes much of Bethel, he makes little of Dan. E is less interested in the official cults of the house of Jeroboam as such than in the various cults under the aegis of Jeroboam's solicited supporters.

INCUBATION

The many dreams in E come from E's interest in incubation. Incubation involves ritual sleep at a sacred shrine. It was a common practice in the ancient world, where it is well attested in Egypt, Mesopotamia, and Greece, as well as Syria and Palestine. The practice in Greece is noteworthy, since it was associated with the shrines of local heroes or holy men or women, as in Palestine.[20] The two main purposes of visiting the Greek shrines were to have mantic dreams and obtain healing.[21] These same purposes apply to Palestine as well. They are seen in the two examples of incubation introduced in the discussion of sons in danger. Danel and Kirta engage in incubation to receive in a dream word about a son, the lack of which was viewed as a physical disability: "Danel, the man of El the *Healer*"; "Kirta was destroyed . . . he had had sons, but . . . one fourth died of disease, one fifth Reshep gathered to himself"; "Abram, the future shrine hero, interceded with God and God *healed* Abimelek and his wife and servants and they bore children."[22]

The best-known example of incubation in the Old Testament is Solomon's dream at Gibeon (1 Kgs 3:4–15). Solomon visited the shrine at Gibeon. There he, like Danel, performed a sacrifice, and then he lay down for the night and dreamed. In the dream, God invited Solomon to make a request. Solomon requested the gift of good judgment. God was pleased with his choice and granted him what he asked. The Deuteronomistic historian has positioned and introduced this incident

---

20. Abram was such a local holy man, in E's conception. Hebrew *nabi*', "holy man, prophet," is used to describe Abram in the first E story. See E. R. Dodds, *The Greeks and the Irrational* (Berkeley: University of California Press, 1951), 107–16, 203 n. 83; Walter Burkert, *Greek Religion* (Cambridge: Harvard University Press, 1985), 190–215.

21. For the medical emphasis, see Dodds, *Greeks and the Irrational*, 115–16; Burkert, *Greek Religion*, 214–15.

22. The recent suggestion that Danel did not in fact sleep or dream seems unlikely, given the parallels; for this suggestion, see Simon B. Parker, "Death and Devotion: The Composition and Theme of *AQHT*," in *Love and Death in the Ancient Near East: Essays in Honor of Marvin H. Pope*, ed. John H. Marks and Robert M. Good (Guilford, Conn.: Four Quarters, 1987), 73 n. 5.

to express disapproval of Solomon's resort to a nontemple shrine (3:2–3). For the sake of centralizing the cult of Yahweh in one place only, the temple in Jerusalem (Deut 12:2–14), the Deuteronomist is suspicious of other cults, particularly those that invite a person to dream or listen to others' dreams: "If a local hero or holy man or woman arises among you, or a dreamer of dreams, and gives you a sign or wonder that comes to pass, and says 'Let's go after other gods,' you shall not listen to the words of that local hero or dreamer of dreams" (Deut 13:1–3).[23] In this Jerusalem court writer's mind, the God of the nontemple shrine dream is likely to be an "other god," of the same ilk as the gods of Bethel as presented by the same historian.

The people of Palestine, however, depended on their local shrines for the sanction of local relations and the adjudication of local disputes in the defense of justice. Men and women resorted to their shrine to sleep there for a dream to confirm their just retribution. The best illustrations of this practice come from the psalms, of which several are complaints prayed in precisely this circumstance. This can usually be recognized even in a standard translation like the Revised Standard Version:

> O Lord, how many are my foes!
> Many are rising against me;
> many are saying of me,
> there is no help for him in God.
> But thou, O Lord, art a shield about me,
> my glory, the lifter of my head.
> I cry aloud to the Lord,
> and he answers me from the hill of his shrine.
> I lie down and sleep;
> I wake again, for the Lord sustains me.
> I am not afraid of ten thousands of people
> who have set themselves against me round about.
> Arise, O Lord!
> Deliver me, O my God!
> For thou dost smite all my enemies on the cheek,
> thou dost break the teeth of the wicked. (Psalm 3)

Psalms 4, 6, 17, and 139 express similar sentiments.[24] The psalmist's cry that "every night I flood my bed with tears, I drench my couch with

---

23. "Dreamer of dreams" is a phrase E uses for Joseph.
24. See Robert B. Coote, "Psalm 139 as Juridical Complaint," in *The Bible and the Politics of Exegesis: Essays in Honor of Norman K. Gottwald*, ed. David Jobling, Peggy Day, and Gerald T. Sheppard (New York: Pilgrim Press, 1991).

my weeping," recalls Kirta's tears pouring "like shekels to the ground,
like fifth-shekels onto his bed" when he was in the same plight.
E is marbled with dreams. From the first scene to the longest, E
refers to fourteen dreams.[25] J referred at most to one or two. Most
dreams in E do not occur at a shrine and therefore do not involve
incubation. Nevertheless, the archetypical dream is Jacob's at Bethel,
and not by chance.[26] Incubation provides the paradigm for dream
revelation in E, in which "interpretations belong to God," and the
numerous dreams in E serve in turn to endorse incubation at the country shrines. The contrast with the Deuteronomist's salvo outlawing
menhirs, shrines, and dreams (Deuteronomy 12–13) could hardly be
sharper. What E and the Deuteronomist together stress is the question
of the country cults' authority, an indication of its critical import for
the monarch.

Another feature of E alludes further to incubation, although it only
occurs half the time in a dream. Recall that one night, as the boy
Samuel lay sleeping at the shrine of Shiloh, God summoned him by
name, "Samuel," or "Samuel, Samuel." Samuel responded to his cult
mentor Eli, "Yes?—Right here" (1 Sam 3:2–9).[27] Although such phatic
usage must have applied in general to a person in authority addressing
a subordinate, its best attestation in the Old Testament suggests a
particular connection with incubation. E shows his interest in such
usage by inserting it as a separate component into the scene of Moses'
first visit to Horeb: "God called out to Moses from the midst of the
bush, 'Moses, Moses,' and he said, 'Yes?—Right here.'" God goes on,
"Take off your sandals, because you are standing at the future shrine
of Horeb." This type of exchange had already occurred four times in E:
to Abram at Beersheba (Gen 22:1), Abram at Moriah (22:11), Jacob in
a dream in Aram (31:11), and Jacob at Beersheba (46:2), including
two of E's three shrine dreams. (Will some future manuscript discovery show it at Gen 28:13 as well, where it would be most expected?)

FEAR

For E, incubation gives access to the protective, yet awesome, God El.
Unlike Yahweh in J, this God who wards his name is no familiar of E's
protagonists. He is formidable, dreadful, a potentate who keeps his

25. The concluding dream occurs during Jacob's incubation at Beersheba.
26. Klein's highlighting of the dream at Bethel is apt ("Ort und Zeit des Elohisten," *Evangelische Theologie* 37 (1977): 248–51). It seems not to be the case, however, that Bethel is the
only shrine at which E narrates a dream (p. 251); Abram and Jacob both have dreams at
Beersheba, the first shrine featured in E, in Gen 22:1–2 (followed by "first thing in the
morning," cf. 20:8; 21:14; 28:18) and 46:1–4.
27. New Revised Standard Version: "Here I am: or "Here am I."

distance—in a word, *fear*some.[28] Access to God is indirect, not direct—as through a dream—and always "from the sky." God does not appear side by side, face to face, or as an unceremonious genie, as Yahweh does in J. Except in a dream, and sometimes even then, God speaks through one of the elite messengers that Jacob spotted running up and down God's palace stairway. It is again no coincidence that of the several times J describes Yahweh standing beside a person to talk, E chooses the one at Bethel to convert into a dream of God's celestial throne room (Gen 28:10–17),[29] underscoring the importance of this theological difference with J by making it most conspicuous at the state shrine. The only face-to-face meeting with God in E occurs in the extraordinary final scene at Horeb: Moses and his chiefs alone see God high on the mountain at Horeb, in God's palace, removed from the common people. On the ground at the same location, Moses had earlier "hid his face because he feared to look at God." In E, it is the royal authority of God, not Solomon, to which people must answer. E's concept of God, however, reflects not only the grave necessity of offsetting the authority of the house of David in Israel with a higher authority but also Jeroboam's desire to reinstate reverential respect for the patron chiefs and magistrates of his realm, as well as for its common law.

In E's view, God and local heroes are encountered near menhirs in the traditional mode of incubation and in the attitude of awed reverence, the "fear" of God, to which E makes nearly a score of references and allusions and that God continuously tests for abatement.[30] Abimelek and his men fear God, though Abram assumed they would not. Abram is prepared to sacrifice Isaac at the place called Fear (Moriah) but is released from this requirement as it becomes evident that he fears God. Jacob awakes with fear and acknowledges the fearsomeness of Bethel. Fearing God, Laban refrains from harming Jacob. Jacob refers to El as the Fearsome God of Isaac. The fear of God prevents harm coming to Jacob and his retinue on their way through the mountains from Shechem to Bethel. Joseph assures his brothers, as he puts them in jeopardy, that he fears God and, thus, that his word is trustworthy.

28. On the motif of fear in E, see Hans Walter Wolff, "The Elohistic Fragments in the Pentateuch," in *The Vitality of Old Testament Traditions*, 2d ed., ed. Walter Brueggemann and Hans Walter Wolff (Atlanta: John Knox, 1982 [German orig. 1969]), 67–82; Jaroš, *Die Stellung des Elohisten*, 45–49.
29. As explained in chap. 1.
30. This motif in E is conveyed in Hebrew by not just the root *yr'* but also *phd, htt, bhl,* and *hrd*—terms for dismay, shaking, and quivering in terror.

E's third part dwells on fearful reverence for judicial process and its integrity. The midwives fear God, not pharaoh's directive. Moses avers that pharaoh will not fear God. The magistrates of Israel fear God, not the wealthy but impious strongmen in Israel nor the house of David, which attempted to bribe and suborn strongmen under Jeroboam. The people of Israel fear God, the author and executor of the laws of Israel. The pervasive motif of fear in E signifies not respect for, and obedience to, Egypt's lawlessness, nor Solomon's, but respect for God's law, kept in the magistrates' cults of Israel and upheld through the magistrates' God-fearing integrity under relentless test: "Blessed is the man who fears God, who takes great delight in his commands" (Ps 112:1).[31]

31. E's notion of the fear of God is not far from that of Proverbs.

CHAPTER TWELVE
Jurisdiction and Law

People prayed for more than sons in the age of Jeroboam I. As the biblical psalms illustrate, they also prayed for the just order implied by the common case law sanctioned by the cults, if not necessarily for the order actually maintained under that law. At the shrines of Israel, people sought law and order, the sacred foundation of every society. The promulgation of a new and written law was the surest sign of a new legal order.[1] Part of Jeroboam's popularity lay in the supposition that laws like E's placed limits on the arbitrary powers of the wealthy patrons of villagers and workers.

LEGAL ORDER

Legal order and sons are not disparate concerns. Law and order is what the solicitude for sons, the menhirs, and the fear of God throughout E all point toward and anticipate. It is a new legal order, and a revolutionary one, requiring the full and exact definition E gives in his concluding collection of case law.[2] A new state cult requires a new legal order. One aspect of the conjunction of menhir cults and legal order appears already in E's description of the agreement between Laban and Jacob, which emphasizes both the menhir

---

1. See Marvin L. Chaney, "Debt Easement in Old Testament History and Tradition," in *The Bible and the Politics of Exegesis: Essays in Honor of Norman K. Gottwald,* ed. David Jobling, Peggy Day, and Gerald T. Sheppard (New York: Pilgrim Press, 1991). On partial parallels to this and other points relating to E's laws in Greek history, see Michael Gagarin, *Early Greek Law* (Berkeley: University of California Press, 1986), esp. chap. 6, "The Emergence of Written Law." Gagarin may overstate the contrast between the ancient Near East and Greece. His emphasis on the role of writing in the official *publication* of newly enacted law applies to E, with certain modifications.
2. For the connection between law and revolution in the medieval and modern history of the West, see Harold J. Berman, *Law and Revolution: The Formation of the Western Legal Tradition* (Cambridge: Harvard University Press, 1983).

and the resolution of the jeopardy to Rachel and Joseph. A second aspect is indicated by a later interpretive supplement to JE already cited: "Moses wrote all the words of Yahweh; then, first thing in the morning, he built an altar at the base of the mountain, along with twelve menhirs, one each for the twelve tribes of Israel" (Exod 24:4)—or their eponymous ancestors. A third aspect concerns lineage directly. The following holy man's oracle, modeled on the formulaic response to a prayer for a son, expresses the link between the birth of a scion and legal order, a basic assumption of the rite of incubation:

> A shoot shall come forth from the root stock of Jesse
>   a branch shall grow from its roots,
> The spirit of Yahweh shall rest on him,
>   the spirit of wisdom and understanding,
>   of counsel and might
>   of loyalty and the *fear of Yahweh* —
>   his delight shall be in the *fear of Yahweh*.
> He shall not judge by what his eyes see,
>   or decide by what his ears hear;
> but with justice he shall judge for the poor,
>   and with fair decision pass judgment for the poor.
> . . . .
> Justice shall be his waist garment,
>   and juridical truth his basic uniform.

The resulting social order will be such that

> The wolf shall dwell beside the lamb,
>   and the leopard shall lie down with the kid.
> . . . .
> They shall not hurt or destroy
>   in all my mountain jurisdiction. (Isa 9:1–9)

As noted, such a son should also erect or patronize a menhir to his ancestor; an aspiring ruler without a son must, like Absalom, arrange for this service himself.

According to the current arrangement of the text describing Solomon's reign, upon his accession he practiced incubation and prayed for good judgment. An editor, possibly as early as the time of Solomon, took one of the psalms to be this prayer:

> A psalm of Solomon:
> Give to the [new] king your judgment, O God,
>   and to the son of the [former] king your justice.
> May he judge your people with justice,
>   your poor with right judgment.

> Let the mountains bear prosperity for the people,
> and the highlands, with justice.
> May he defend the cause of the poor,
> deliver the poor,
> and crush the oppressor. (Ps 72:1–4)

One of the sons for whom Kirta so fervently prayed later charges that Kirta has neglected justice. The son contends he can do better and complains to his father,

> Weakness has stayed your hand:
> You do not judge the cases of widows,
> you do not preside over the hearings of the
> oppressed;
> you do not drive out those who plunder the poor,
> you do not feed the fatherless before you,
> the widow behind you.
> The sickbed has become your brother,
> the stretcher your close friend.
> Come down from the kingship—let me be king,
> from your power—let me sit on the throne.[3]

The assumption that the magistrate's son continues his father's practice of justice or rights his father's injustice is the keystone of E's notion of social order.

CULT AND JURISDICTION

For E, the fear of God who saves sons connotes judicial integrity. The basis of legal order and jurisdiction for E was the common law of the state and country cults, at the heart of Jeroboam's organized, decentralized jurisdiction. With his version of this law, which in the north was common to town and village, E constructs his final episode, the goal to which all in E tends.

E's conception of rule has the appearance of being so opposed to tyranny as to establish a government of laws, not men, as though E were an early John Locke. He is not, although, as in Locke's context, there certainly are embedded in E concessions to a landowning class whose interests limit those of the monarch. As indicated in chapter 6, what E reflects is the difference in the typical structure of law in the Israelite and Jerusalemite highlands, due to their different social structures. In Judah, one law applied in Jerusalem and another outside. This

---

3. Michael David Coogan, *Stories from Ancient Canaan* (Philadelphia: Westminster, 1978), 73–74. Coogan (pp. 54–55) notes the similarity to Absalom's challenge to David in 2 Samuel 15.

is reflected in Absalom's setting up court at Jerusalem's gate to adjudicate cases in terms the country folk hold valid (2 Sam 15:2–6), and in the absence from J of case law. In Israel, the same law tended to apply in both Shechem (or a subsequent capital) and the countryside. This is reflected in Ahab's pained acquiescence in the law of inalienability appealed to by Naboth (1 Kgs 21:1–4).

The king of Israel normally regarded himself as subject to the laws of the nation. E's purpose is not to create this relationship but to incorporate it, as a given. This legal relationship fits E's broad confirmation of Israel's strongmen and magistrates in their role as household heads and judicial arbiters, and of Israel's cults as the locus of this role—all in support of the revolution that resonated with Jeroboam's personal rise to power. For Jeroboam, Israel's law stood for more than the popular rebuff of lawless Solomon. In Jeroboam's Israel, the execution of state law was a cornerstone of strongmen's power. This is the reason law receives the emphasis it does in E.[4]

The role of the cult in jurisdiction—a somewhat impenetrable notion in societies dedicated to the supposed separation of church and state, such as the United States—is perhaps best illustrated by the exclusive attention paid in Psalm 15 (paraphrased here) to the ultimate value associated with the sanctuary—truth in juridical witness:[5]

> O God, who shall sojourn in your tent? Who shall dwell on your holy hill? Whoever proceeds in the plain truth, and executes justice, and utters the truth in their mind; whoever does not slander with the tongue, nor makes false charge against neighbor; in whose eyes a reprobate is despised, but who honors those who *fear God;* who swear to their own hurt in trial without flinching, who do not themselves put out money at exorbitant interest, and who do not take a bribe against the innocent. Whoever does these things shall stand fast in the sanctuary of God.

The local shrine makes its appearance at several points in E's collection of laws: "His master shall have him *approach God,*"[6] "I shall designate a *shrine* to which he may flee," "The owner of the house

4. Some have argued that prior to Omri, Israel was more a chiefdom than a state. Further research may determine whether the difference in political organization between Israel and Judah in this period was based more on their inherent social and legal structures or their political evolution.
5. This subject, evident in all parts of the Bible, is a significant theme in Robert B. Coote and Mary P. Coote, *Power, Politics, and the Making of the Bible* (Minneapolis: Fortress, 1990), *s. v.* "Jurisdiction," but it requires in addition its own separate and detailed treatment.
6. The juridical sense of the Hebrew phrase "to God" is clear from E's use of the expression in Exod 18:19.

shall be brought *to God,*" and "Both parties shall present their case *before God.*"

As observed by many others, E dwells on the niceties of a case. In E, "sin," more frequently mentioned than in J, usually means breaking the law. Is Abimelek guilty of wife stealing? Is Abram guilty of deception? Is Abimelek guilty of encroaching on someone else's water? Does young Joseph have a right to part of Laban's wealth? Is Jacob guilty of theft? Is Joseph guilty of rape? Are Joseph's brothers guilty of kidnapping? Does Moses have the right to lead his people out of Egypt? E elaborates on the evidence to answer such questions not because he holds a particular view of history or human nature, or of what makes a good story, but because the entire narrative points toward the application of case law, which requires just such attention to the ins and outs of a case.

E'S LAW

In theory at least, E's law limits the prerogatives of the landed magistracy to make laws, as opposed to applying them. It also ameliorates the injustices of the ruler who does not have to make such allowances to a powerful magistracy. E's case law reflects the quasi-tribal polity Jeroboam wants or is willing, in part, to restore. In contrast to cuneiform law from more powerful and autonomous courts, E's law makes a distinction between accidental killing and murder; never stipulates the death penalty for a violation of property rights alone; limits retribution to a corresponding injury, thus excluding excessive and vicarious punishments (the lex talionis, or law limiting revenge); and does not recognize class differences as such in setting penalties.[7] Nevertheless, the hierarchy of jurisdiction conceived by E borders on the military.[8] Magistrates are appointed for overlapping units of twenty, fifty,

7. Moshe Greenberg, "Crimes and Punishments," in *Interpreter's Dictionary of the Bible,* ed. George Arthur Buttrick et al. (Nashville: Abingdon, 1962), 1: 735. For recent treatments of law in E, see Shalom M. Paul, *Studies in the Book of the Covenant in the Light of Cuneiform and Biblical Law* (Leiden: E. J. Brill, 1970); Hans Jochen Boecker, *Law and the Administration of Justice in the Old Testament and Ancient East* (Minneapolis: Augsburg, 1980); Dale Patrick, *Old Testament Law* (Atlanta: John Knox, 1985), 63–96; Frank Crüsemann, "Das Bundesbuch—historischer Ort und institutioneler Hintergrund," in *Congress Volume: Jerusalem, 1988,* supp. to *Vetus Testamentum* 40, ed. J. A. Emerton (Leiden: E. J. Brill, 1988); Raymond Westbrook, *Property and the Family in Biblical Law* (Sheffield: Sheffield University Press, 1990); Meir Malul, *The Comparative Method in Ancient Near Eastern and Biblical Legal Studies* (Neukirchen-Vluyn: Neukirchner Verlag/Kevelaer: Butzon and Bercker, 1990).
8. E's jurisdictional hierarchy looks like the organization of the levy for forced labor (for which Jeroboam once bore responsibility) and the military. See Keith W. Whitelam, *The Just King: Monarchical Judicial Authority in Ancient Israel* (Sheffield: JSOT Press, 1979), 193–94; Robert R. Wilson, "Israel's Judicial System in the Preexilic Period," *The Jewish Quarterly Review* 74 (1983): 229–48.

one hundred, and one thousand family heads. Under this arrangement, organization can be tight, allowing for little deviation and fostering a species of revolutionary discipline.[9] The collection of laws that concludes E is not a "code," or rationalized, systematic treatment of the entire range of circumstances that might arise in the society governed by Jeroboam and his men. However, it does group laws loosely according to certain conventional categories of ancient Near Eastern law. If the collection is not a code, what is it? In the ancient Near East, there was a tradition by which kings occasionally promulgated sets of laws that both publicized the ruler's intent to stay the erosion of justice and provided examples of what the ruler regarded as standards for equitable adjudication.[10] E's set of laws does not cover all contingencies any more than individual laws cover all the situations illustrated in E's narrative. However, it is supposed to cover enough to convey an idea of how to arrive at a right decision in a case not covered.

Whether Jeroboam's magistrates had access to this collection of laws is another question. Thousands of legal documents contemporaneous with sets of cuneiform law never refer to those sets and often differ from their rules. Indeed, "even the kings who publish them take no special notice of them in their historical records."[11] Cuneiform law sets seem not to have been written for judges or officials but for gods or human posterity to read, so they could recognize how just the ruler was. This should give us pause. E's law, however, does not appear to follow the cuneiform pattern. E's laws could be read along with the rest of E to visiting strongmen in Jeroboam's court. Short sets could be written on stone, or in plaster on stone, for public display at a cult site. These would then exemplify the legal basis of state order, and a judge not already familiar with the royal court's ruling or tendency on a

---

9. I owe this insight to Boikanyo C. Maaga. Rolf Knierim ("Exodus 18 und die Neuordnung der mosaischen Gerichtsbarkeit," *Zeitschrift für die alttestamentliche Wissenschaft* 73 [1961]: 146–71) argues that Exodus 18 in its present form provides an explanation for Jehoshaphat's reform described in 2 Chr 19:4–11. The Deuteronomist, of course, makes much of the system of jurisdiction laid down by E (Deut 1:9–18; 16:18–20; 17:8–13) and at the same time denounces the cult menhir: "You shall not erect for yourself a menhir, because Yahweh your God hates them" (Deut 16:22). The Deuteronomist takes centralization to its logical extreme, an option Jeroboam could not afford. E follows J in making Moses—possibly a northern chief in the first place—rather than the king the deliverer of the law.

10. Research continues on this important topic. Recent summaries include Niels P. Lemche, "*Andurarum* and *Mišarum*: Comments on the Problem of Social Edicts and Their Application in the Ancient Near East," *Journal of Near Eastern Studies* 38 (1979): 11–22; F. R. Kraus, *Königliche Verfügungen in altbabylonischer Zeit* (Leiden: E. J. Brill, 1984); Raymond Westbrook, "Biblical and Cuneiform Law Codes," *Revue Biblique* 92 (1985): 247–64. See especially Chaney, "Debt Easement in Old Testament History."

11. Samuel Greengus, "Law in the OT," in *Interpreter's Dictionary of the Bible*, supp. vol., ed. Keith Crim (Nashville: Abindgon, 1976), 534.

question could use them for comparison. Treaty texts are known to have been displayed in this way, legal sections and all. It is reasonable to suppose that at least part of E's collection of laws appeared displayed on stone tablets or filed in parchment scrolls at the shrines named in E.

E's collection follows essentially the same categories of laws found in other ancient Near Eastern collections. These include evidence, property (theft, transfer, damage, safekeeping, and the like), marriage and family, and bodily injury. E's most distinctive group of laws is the first, relating to debt slavery, which was similar, though not identical, to what we know as indentured service.[12] There appears to have been in ancient Near Eastern law no regular topical division concerned with slaves, of which more than one kind existed. Slave laws were included under other rubrics, including family law, theft, bodily injury, and miscellaneous addenda. In the extant collections, slave laws tend to be scattered in the later parts or at the end.[13]

E's placement of slave laws at the beginning is an unusual departure from the norm. What is the reason? Perhaps E put slave laws first because the limitation on the term of slavery to seven years, although following precedent, would be popular with the people whose freedoms had been jeopardized for so many years by Solomon's policies. However, the main audience of this collection were more liable to own slaves than be slaves. The content of the laws suggests a different reason for their placement. The slave laws deal with a father's loss of sons and daughters, E's obsession. Fathers can lose their sons and daughters as slaves, and slaves can lose their own sons and daughters. To keep his wife and sons, a slave may sign on for life, in a rite carried out at the local shrine. This law supports both the slave family and the slave owner and as such is a fitting legal, as well as symbolic, spearhead for the legal interests of Jeroboam's court.[14]

The relationship between the fear of God and the limitation of debt slavery is illustrated by an enactment by Nehemiah in response to the enslavement of Judahites by Judahites for debt (Nehemiah 5). "We are

---

12. Dale Patrick, *Old Testament Law* (Atlanta: John Knox, 1985), 70.
13. See Stephen A. Kaufman, "The Second Table of the Decalogue and the Implicit Categories of Ancient Near Eastern Law," in *Love and Death in the Ancient Near East: Essays in Honor of Marvin H. Pope*, ed. John H. Marks and Robert M. Good (Guilford, Conn.: Four Quarters, 1987), 111–16. Many historians have thought that the Decalogue, Exod 20:2–17, belongs to E; I regard this as unlikely, given that there are no distinctive features of E in the Decalogue, and it fills no apparent structural purpose in E.
14. See Niels P. Lemche, "'The Hebrew Slave': Comments on the Slave Law Ex. 21: 2–11," *Vetus Testamentum* 25 (1975): 129–44; Timothy John Turnbaum, "Male and Female Slaves in the Sabbath Year Laws of Exodus 21:1–11," *Society of Biblical Literature 1987 Seminar Papers* (Atlanta: Scholars Press, 1987), 545–49.

mortgaging our fields, vineyards, and houses," men were saying, "to get grain because of the famine. We have borrowed money for the royal tax on our fields and vineyards. We are having to give up our sons and daughters as slaves, and we can't help ourselves because other men now own our fields and vineyards." Nehemiah indicted the Judahite kulaks and then added, "What you are doing is not good. You should walk instead in the *fear of God.* Give back immediately the people's fields, vineyards, olive orchards, and houses, and the money, grain, wine, and oil you have been exacting from them." Nehemiah maintained further that "previous governors laid heavy burdens on the people, and took from them food and wine, and forty shekels of silver. I, however, did no such thing, because of the *fear of God.*"

The law speaks of a "Hebrew" slave. "Hebrew" does not simply designate a citizen of Israel or a member of a uniform ethnic group, as it continues to be understood despite much recent research. The term translated "Hebrew" designated an uprooted or migrant Palestinian.[15] It continued to be used of Israelite Palestinians to the end of the tenth century B.C.E. and later because of the social upheaval and uprooted-ness of laborers brought on under David's and Solomon's rule, and again under Omri in Israel. The debt slave was by definition an up-rooted worker. Although Jacob is not, strictly speaking, a debt slave, his status as a worker for Laban is similar; thus, E has Jacob go on at length about the harsh conditions of his work and unsympathetic dom-ination by his master.

E supplements J extensively at a point that J and E both regard as fundamental but of which J makes comparatively little: the cultic promulgation of law. J presented the law of the cult (the law covering cult behavior); E presents the cult's law (the whole law sanctioned by the cult). The subject of cultic law could hardly be overexpounded, as shown by later amplifications that ballooned this section of the Tetrateuch.

It is at just this point that most of the additions to JE from Hezekiah, king of the house of David in the late eighth century B.C.E., are to be found. The Deuteronomist adopted E's description of jurisdiction (Ex-odus 18) for the opening scene of the entire Deuteronomistic history (Deut 1:9–18). Then he placed Josiah's corresponding state cult's nor-mative edicts and case laws in the history's opening scroll and made those laws—in the form of the vital, but misplaced, document contain-ing Moses' legal instruction (New Revised Standard Version: "book of

---

15. Nadav Na'aman, "Habiru and Hebrews: The Transfer of a Social Term to the Literary Sphere," *Journal of Near Eastern Studies* 45 (1986): 271–88.

the law")—the overarching theme of the entire history. The priestly editors of the Tetrateuch expanded E's cultic and legal additions to J by twenty times or more and made them, by literary design and sheer weight, more clearly than ever the objective of universal history. It is no accident, and should occasion no surprise, that with Jeroboam's cult law, E draws his contribution to the official history of Israel to a climactic close—to be reopened two hundred years later by Hezekiah.

CHAPTER THIRTEEN

Hezekiah's JE

The basic circumstances leading to J, E, and P were simple, but the additional sedimentation, folding, and faulting that produced the finished Tetrateuch were complex indeed. It is not always possible to identify the historical context in which a text not in J, E, or P was added. Such texts are particularly common in Exodus and Numbers. Much can be said about the Ten Commandments from a historical perspective, but exactly how and why they got into the Tetrateuch is not known.[1] The intriguing pair of texts in Exod 19:3–8 and 24:3–8 is likewise difficult to place historically. One group of texts whose origin does seem clear is a group that shares characteristics with both J and the Deuteronomistic history, a possible indication that it is to be located somehow between them. Nearly all the texts in this group appear to be added to E, and they are sometimes included in lists of E passages. It is thus necessary to examine these texts briefly.

ASSYRIAN DOMINANCE

The texts under consideration come from Jerusalem and display a style and promote views reminiscent of both J and the Deuteronomistic tradition. They could have been added to the Tetrateuch after it was joined to the Deuteronomistic history, sometime in the late sixth or fifth century B.C.E. Or they could have been added by a forerunner of the Deuteronomist. Given their intermediate character between J and the Deuteronomist, the latter alternative seems more likely. Evidence indicates that Hezekiah launched a reform that anticipated

1. See chap. 12, n. 13.

Josiah's Deuteronomistic reform.[2] Hezekiah supported a vigorous
scriptorium. He solicited Israelites and therefore had reason to substitute for the Jerusalem version of J its Israelite counterpart, JE. Thus,
the group of texts being considered was probably added to JE in the
court of Hezekiah. They may be regarded as proto-Deuteronomistic.
With the fall of Samaria in 722 B.C.E., the six hundred years of the
history of Israel as a tribal and state polity ended. The people of Israel
were still there, except for most of an entire generation of the ruling
class, who were reestablished elsewhere in the Assyrian Empire.
Without a ruling class, there was no more Israelite "national" identity.
The Israelite rulers were replaced with men and their families deported from other parts of the Assyrian empire. Samaria and Megiddo
were the only cities known to be left fortified. At other city sites,
shrunken unwalled settlements housed the displaced. At Hazor,
the Assyrians built a palace fortress on the abandoned citadel. Northeast of the citadel, a new town grew up around the turn of the seventh
century. Its monumental buildings were modeled on the palaces of
Syria and Assyria. Assyrian pottery imports and copies became common, and other Assyrian stone and metal artifacts were imitated.

The Israelite villagers of Palestine, now under Assyrian rule, carried
on as before. The traditional pillared house was increasingly replaced
by the Assyrian house, consisting of a courtyard with rooms on all
sides. The Assyrian administration supported the cults of both Yahweh
and the gods and goddesses of the replacement elites. Adherents of the
cult of Yahweh in the central and northern sections of Palestine still
called themselves Israelites. As expected, Shechem again became their
center, although they lived throughout the territory. The Assyrian
governor kept Bethel going as a border cult, much as in the days of
Jeroboam I. The house of David, however, reclaimed the native rule
of Israel, which in their view had been illegally expropriated by Jeroboam I, even while the house of David was vassal to Assyria.

The century following the fall of Samaria was the great age of the
Assyrian Empire. A single dynasty held sway, the renowned ruling
house of Sargon II, comprising Sargon, Sennacherib, Esarhaddon, and
Ashurbanipal. In Judah, the house of David was ruled by two long-
reigning kings, Hezekiah (715–687) and his son Manasseh (696–642).
During most of this period, the house of David was an Assyrian vassal.
The longevity of the two Assyrian Davidids had as much to do with

2. The issue is still under discussion. The best case for the view followed here is made by
Jonathan Rosenbaum, "Hezekiah's Reform and the Deuteronomistic Tradition," *Harvard
Theological Review* 72 (1979): 23–43.

Assyrian machination as with their own ability, health, and luck. The house of David was independent in name only.

Hezekiah succeeded Ahaz in 715 and, in agreement with his father's treaty, held his peace with Sargon.[3] Sargon (722–705) organized trade with Egypt and stimulated commercial relations all over Palestine by moving groups to new settlements and disrupting longstanding social relations. Coastal cities like Ashdod grew in size and splendor. Palestinian and North Arabian tribes were corralled: "I crushed the tribes of Tamud, Ibadidi, Marsimanu, and Haiapa, the Arabs who live far away in the desert and who know neither overseers nor officials, and who had not brought their tribute to any king; I deported their survivors and settled them in Samarina [Israel]." With control of the southern land routes, Sargon received homage and gifts from the monarchs of the Hijaz and South Arabia, whose states grew as extensions of Assyrian hegemony. The age-old Assyrian goal of control of the eastern Mediterranean was achieved. The kings of Cyprus paid tribute to Assyria beginning in 709. Imported Greek pottery became increasingly common along the coast.

HEZEKIAH'S RESISTANCE AND REFORM

Sargon's rule on the Palestine coast did not go undisputed, despite powerful Assyrian occupation forces. The king of Ashdod, Azuri, rebelled in 713 and brought in the coastal towns of Gath and Asdudimmu with him. An attempt was made to implicate Egypt as well, where the pharaoh had made anti-Assyrian probes into the Sinai. Sargon ordered Azuri's brother installed in his stead. The insurgent party deposed this Assyrian puppet and put an Aegean strongman in his place. In 712, Sargon, furious at this insubordination, marched his palace guard all the way to Ashdod, laid siege to the defiant cities, captured them, sacked the Aegean's household, and reorganized the cities' administration under a new and more powerful Assyrian officer. The other coastal towns, along with Judah, Edom, and Moab, sent gifts reaffirming their loyalty to the Assyrian god Ashur. The Aegean fled to Egypt. When the outcome became clear, however, the pharaoh extradited him to Sargon. Hezekiah sat out this revolt.

3. Two recent studies independently propose to date Hezekiah's accession at 727 B.C.E.: Mordechai Cogan and Hayim Tadmor, *2 Kings: A New Translation with Introduction and Commentary* (New York: Doubleday, 1988); John H. Hayes and Paul K. Hooker, *A New Chronology for the Kings of Israel and Judah and Its Implications for Biblical History and Literature* (Atlanta: John Knox, 1988). For now, the date usually given seems more likely.

Sargon died in 705 while defending the empire against Asian tribes to the northeast. His son and successor, Sennacherib (705–681), rivaled his father in power and grandeur. Sennacherib left Sargon's new capital of Dur-sharrukin (Khorsabad) as a mere fortress, rebuilt the ancient city of Nineveh on a huge scale, and made it the Assyrian capital. Before long, Sennacherib had a region-wide revolt on his hands, headed by Merodach-baladan of Babylon, with Babylonian and Aramaean tribes and Elam as co-conspirators. He sent embassies to the west and acquired the backing of Hezekiah and other kings on and near the coast, including the kings of Tyre, Ammon, Moab, and Edom. These kings saw the chance to exchange a strong Assyrian overlord for a weaker Babylonian one, or to weaken both by supporting their fight with one another. Egypt joined in under Shebitku.

Hezekiah braced himself for the struggle with Assyria. Hand in hand with his administrative and military preparations went the reform of the royal temple cult, a standard device by which a monarch could establish or reassert authority. Hezekiah refurbished Solomon's temple. Assyrians had disorganized the internal political configuration of Judah in order to weaken the house of David without altogether bringing it down. Sargon was not limited to dealing with Hezekiah alone in trying to keep Judah from interfering with his control of the coast. As the Assyrians bought and extorted allegiance from Judahite strongmen, the support of local holy men and women, hitherto largely ignored by the house of David, grew more important to Hezekiah. Ahaz's counselor Isaiah, a Jerusalemite worthy now an old man, commended the king's reform and, as an outcome of the crisis, looked for the reign of justice predicated in the temple's scriptures. This was enough for Hezekiah, and he suppressed other local heroes in favor of Isaiah.

Hezekiah moved to restore support in the land by centralizing the nation's cult, along with its administration. He acted on the house of David's claim to Israel by appealing to the north to participate in a national cult of Jerusalem. He named his firstborn son Manasseh as a token of his good faith toward Israel, and he accommodated the Israelite agricultural calendar by scheduling the pilgrimage feast of Passover one month later than on the Judahite calendar.

A central cult entailed central jurisdiction. Laws were promulgated that reinforced the prerogatives of Jerusalem: "You shall not permit an unauthorized holy woman to live. . . . Whoever sacrifices to any god other than [Jerusalemite] Yahweh shall be destroyed." Under Assyrian influence and order, the population of Judah had become unusually varied, and all the support possible was needed—therefore, "You shall not wrong a stranger or oppress him." Hezekiah sought the support of the village populace for the monarch and against their local lords, who in any case were susceptible to bribes from abroad—therefore, "If you lend money to any poor, you shall not exact interest." The local cults, sanctioning local jurisdictions not under Hezekiah's control, were outlawed. Excavations at Arad in southern Judah indicate that its temple was destroyed at this time.

Hezekiah helped to weaken pro-Assyrian forces on the coast. Luli, king of Sidon, who ruled the coast from Sidon to Akko, including Tyre, rebelled. Sidqia usurped the throne of Ashkelon, which controlled the port of Joppa as well, and rebelled. The notables of Ekron overthrew their Assyrian-appointed king, Padi, and turned him over to Hezekiah for incarceration. This move strengthened Hezekiah's claims over coastal territory. From this base Hezekiah attacked Gaza and its king Sillibel, who held out against joining the rebellion. Gath fell into Hezekiah's hands.

Hezekiah's preparations for the Assyrian siege did much to keep Judah in royal hands during the height of Assyrian power in Palestine. Hezekiah selected cities in the Judahite hills and foothills, strengthened their fortifications, stored extra weapons and provisions in them, and provided them with reinforced garrisons. High-quality jars stamped with a royal symbol, the label *lmlk* (royal property), and the name of one of four towns were manufactured in a single foothill center and distributed around the realm. These were filled with produce contributed by all sectors of the population and then sent on to the fortified cities. The attack was expected from the north and west. The area covered by the defense system was divided into four districts: the foothills and the southern, central, and northern hills. Hebron, one of the four towns named on the provision jars, was the center of the system. (The purpose of the other three towns is not known.)[4]

Jerusalem, already well fortified, received special attention. The city wall was reinforced. The great Israelite cities had installed mammoth tunnels to their springs during the ninth century. Jerusalem's main spring, however, still lay outside the eastern wall. Hezekiah ordered a tunnel cut through solid rock beneath the city to a pool within the wall at the south end. To finish the tunnel fast, it was dug from both ends at once. The joining of the two excavations was an engineering feat of the first order. It was commemorated by a description inscribed on the wall ten yards inside the southern end of the tunnel, which is the longest early Hebrew inscription known.

---

4. Nadav Na'aman, "Hezekiah's Fortified Cities and the *LMLK* Stamps," *Bulletin of the American Schools of Oriental Research* 261 (1986): 5–21.

HEZEKIAH'S "VICTORY"

Hezekiah's defenses gave way to the Assyrian onslaught. Egypt's expeditionary force was ravaged. Sennacherib's stonecutters made the capture of Lachish the centerpiece of their depiction of the conquest of Judah in reliefs carved on the palace walls in Nineveh. Lachish had been refounded about two hundred years earlier, probably under the rule of Rehoboam. It had a huge wall with a mighty gate and was surrounded by a revetted earthen ramp designed to hamper siege machinery. Inside the walls was a palace fortress, the most massive building yet uncovered from the entire monarchic period in Palestine. Hezekiah's agents at Lachish were captured and beheaded or flayed alive. The city's people were forced to march to Nineveh. There the lower classes were put to work in the crews building Sennacherib's palace. The warriors were incorporated into the palace bodyguard as a Judahite regiment in native uniform.

Once Lachish was taken, the rest of the land lay open for conquest. Sennacherib's chronicle of the event boasted that he attacked "forty-six of his strong cities, walled forts, and the countless small villages in their vicinity. [I] conquered them by means of well-stamped earth-ramps, and battering rams brought thus near to the walls combined with the attack by foot soldiers, using mines, breeches, as well as sapper work. [I] drove out 200, 150 people, young and old, male and female, along with horses, mules, donkeys, camels, sheep, goats, and cattle beyond counting, and considered them booty."[5]

Sennacherib's account concluded with the siege of Jerusalem: "Hezekiah I made prisoner in Jerusalem, his royal residence, like a bird in a cage. I surrounded him with earthwork in order to molest those who were leaving his city's gate."[6] Hezekiah bought off Sennacherib before the city was taken. With Sennacherib directing the siege of Jerusalem from quarters at Lachish, Hezekiah sent word he would capitulate.

Sennacherib turned the lands of the captured towns and villages over to the kings of Ashdod, Ekron, and Gaza, thereby enlarging the fiefs of his clients in the Philistine plain on the frontier with Egypt. Hezekiah's troops in Jerusalem, whose provision was tied to these lands, abandoned him for new masters. "Thus I reduced his country," Sennacherib pointed out, "but I still increased the tribute and gifts due to

5. James B. Pritchard, *Ancient Near Eastern Texts Relating to the Old Testament* (Princeton: Princeton University Press, 1955), 288.
6. Ibid.

me as overlord which I imposed upon him beyond the initial tribute, to be delivered annually."[7] The first tribute was colossal. In addition to thirty talents of gold and eight hundred talents of silver, there were gems; antimony; jewels; beds and chairs with ivory inlay; elephant hides and tusks; maple; boxwood; woolen and linen garments; dyed wool; vessels of copper, iron, bronze, and lead; iron; chariots; shields; lances; armor; iron daggers; bows and arrows; and spears. Hezekiah also had to give up his daughters, palace womenservants, and musicians. The cult he had attempted to make preeminent was greatly weakened. Judah was engulfed by Assyria and remained in its grip for the following seventy years.

Sennacherib counted his booty from the other captured cities at ten thousand bows and ten thousand shields, which he added to his own armory. Thousands of captives were distributed as slaves to the captains of his army and other imperial strongmen.

By the time Sennacherib had withdrawn, the fortified towns in the foothills and to the northwest of Jerusalem had been devastated. Hebron and the Judahite plateau, however, had not been taken. These were left to the dismantled house of David. Given this family's traditional authority in Jerusalem, a compliant Hezekiah remained the Assyrians' best bet for stable rule in the Judahite mountains. Most of Judah remained in his hands as Assyrian vassal. Jerusalem grew. Hezekiah expanded the walls to enclose two new quarters to the west. This new area was not so much for supposed refugees from Israel as for the expanding population of Judah during the height of the Assyrian period.

Hezekiah presided over the loss to the house of David of control of the trade route from Elat to Gaza. There the Assyrians found better allies in the Arab tribes. These benefited from Assyrian trade and work and helped Assyria against Egypt during the reign of Hezekiah's son Manasseh.

SCRIPTURE REVISIONS

Hezekiah turned his trial and purchase of Jerusalem's rescue into a propaganda victory. Jerusalem had been threatened with the fate of Samaria but had been delivered. As Hezekiah and his court presented it, this event confirmed the righteousness of the house of David. The fall of Samaria became for the temple establishment of Jerusalem the sign and seal of their own legitimacy. The Davidic

---

7. Ibid.

program of forming one nation out of Israel and Judah lay at the heart of Hezekiah's pretensions. The court reappropriated David's J in its northern supplemented form and made its own slight revisions in a prototype of the amalgam of Jerusalemite scriptural style, traditional Israelite idiom, and contemporary clerical wording that historians call Deuteronomistic.

The texts of this revision that fall within the scope of E follow in italics:[8]

Because Yahweh had indeed closed all the wombs of the house of Abimelek because of Saray, Abram's wife. . .

Abram planted a tamarisk in Beersheba and invoked there the name of Yahweh, El eternal. . .

Abram named that shrine "Yahweh-Sees," as the saying goes today, "On the mount of Yahweh he will be seen."[9] *The genie of Yahweh called to Abram again from the sky, "I have sworn—utterance of Yahweh— that because you have performed this act and not withheld your one and only son I shall most assuredly bless you and make your descendants as numerous as the stars of the sky and as the sand on the seashore. Your descendants shall possess the gates of their enemies. All the nations of the earth shall gain blessing through your descendants, since you heeded my voice." Abram returned then to his boys, and they went together back to Beersheba, where Abram stayed. . . .*

And Yahweh will become my God. . .

whom I gave as slave to my husband. . .

[You do not yet fear] *Yahweh* [God]. . .

Amalek came and fought with Israel in Rephidim. Moses said to Joshua, "Choose men and go out and do battle with Amalek: tomorrow I am going to be stationed on the top of the hill, with the God-rod in my hand." Joshua went out to do battle as Moses told him, while Moses, Aaron, and Hur went to the top of the hill. Then whenever Moses raised his hand, Israel would prevail, but whenever he lowered his hand, Amalek prevailed. When Moses' arms became tired, they sat him on a stone. Then Aaron on one side and Hur on the other held up Moses' hands, which were held steady until sundown. Thus Joshua vanquished Amalek and his men by the sword. Yahweh said to Moses, "Record this as a memorial in a document, and make sure Joshua gets the point, for I have erased the memory of Amalek from beneath the sky." Moses built an altar and called it "Yahweh is my banner"; he said, "[   ]; Yahweh is perpetually at war with Amalek". . . .

8. See the list of texts at the end of this book.
9. Or "it shall be provided."

Hezekiah's Laws

"You shall not permit an unauthorized holy woman to live. Anyone who lies with an animal shall be executed. Anyone who makes sacrifice to gods other than Yahweh [of Jerusalem] shall be destroyed.

"You shall not wrong a resident stranger or oppress him, for you were resident strangers in Egypt. You shall not oppress a widow or fatherless son. If you do oppress them, and they cry out to me, I will hear their cry and get angry and kill you with the sword, and your own wives will become widows and sons, fatherless.

"If you lend money to my people, the poor among you, you shall not behave as a moneylender. You shall not exact interest from him. If you have to take your neighbor's clothes in pledge, give them back to him when the sun goes down—it's his only covering, his garment for his skin. What else is he going to sleep in? If he cries out to me, I am going to hear him, because I am merciful.

"You shall not revile God, nor curse a chief of your people [who conduct the cult for Yahweh]: you must measure your contribution on the basis of your whole harvest and total output of wine and oil. Your firstborn son you must give to me. You must do the same with your herds and flocks. Seven days the firstborn may be with its mother. On the eighth, you must give it to me.

"You must be men sanctified for me. You must not eat meat torn up in the field. Throw it to the dog.

"You shall not pass on slanderous hearsay in court. You shall not conspire with bad men to present wrongful witness. You shall not pervert justice by following the crowd. Nor shall you [   ] when the poor man brings suit.

"If you come across your enemy's ox or ass gone astray, you must return it to him. If you see the ass of someone you are on poor terms with [   ].

"You shall not pervert the justice due the poor in his suit. Stay away from false testimony. Don't end up responsible for the death of some clean and innocent man. I will not hold the guilty party guiltless. Take no bribe. Bribes cause blindness and drain the substance from the testimony of the innocent.

"Do not oppress a resident stranger. You know the needs of the resident stranger, because you were resident strangers in Egypt.

"Sow your land for six years, and gather in its produce. In the seventh year, leave it alone, so your poor can eat from it. The wild animals can eat what's left over. Do the same with your vineyard and olive grove.

"For six days do your work. Rest on the seventh day, so that your ox and ass can rest, and your slave and resident strangers can take a breather.

"Pay close attention to everything I have said to you.

"Invoke the name of no other gods — don't let them so much as cross your lips. Three times a year you shall make a pilgrimage to my shrine. Keep the pilgrimage holiday of unleavened bread. For seven days eat unleavened bread, as I commanded you for the feast of the month of Abib, since that's when you left Egypt. Do not come empty-handed. Keep the pilgrimage holiday of the wheat harvest, the earliest crop of what you sowed in the fall. And the pilgrimage holiday of the harvest of fruit, olives, and nuts, at the end of the year, when you harvest what you have worked on in your fields.

"Three times a year all your men folk shall visit the shrine of your sovereign, Yahweh. Do not sacrifice blood for me with leavened bread, and do not let the fat of my pilgrimage feasts last until morning. The first of the fruits of your land you shall bring to the temple of Yahweh your God.

"You shall not boil a kid in its mother's milk.

Judicial Warnings

"I am sending a guardian genie before you to guard you on the way and bring you safely to the shrine I have established. Watch out for him, and do what he says. Do not rebel against him. He won't forgive your disobedience, for my [judicial] name is in him. If you do listen to him, and do everything I tell you, I will make your enemies my enemies, and your adversaries mine.

"When my genie goes before you and brings you to the Amorite, Hittite, Perizzite, Canaanite, Hivite, and Jebusite, and I destroy them, do not bow down to their gods, or work for or serve them, or do as they do. Do not fail to tear down their gods and smash up their menhirs. Work for and serve Yahweh your God, and he will bless your food and water and remove sickness from you. None shall suffer miscarriage or remain childless in your land, and everyone shall live out their normal life span.

"I shall send terror in your van, and cast into confusion all those amongst whom you shall come, and make all your enemies offer their neck to your foot. I will send hornets in your van, and they shall drive away from you the Hivite, Canaanite, and Hittite. I won't drive them away from you in one year, lest the land become desolate and the wild animals multiply too quickly. Little by little I will drive them away from you, until you are sufficiently fruitful to take full possession of

your grant. And I will extend the boundaries of your territory from Sup Sea to the Philistine Sea, and from the desert to the Euphrates. For I will deliver the strongmen of the land into your hands, and you shall drive them away from you. You shall not make a covenant with them or their gods. Don't allow them any land in your country, lest they cause you to break my law. Make no mistake: if you work for or serve their gods, you will be snared. . . ."
[Moses arose] *with Joshua his servant* [and Moses went up to the mountain of God.] *To the sheikhs he said, "Sit here until we come back. Aaron and Hur are with you. If you have a case you can't handle, tell it to them."*[10]

HEZEKIAH'S JE

Hezekiah's adoption of JE in place of J, again as a mirror to the interests of his court, served both to rally support against Assyria, in JE symbolized by Egypt, and to foster support of Assyria in its suzerainty of Palestine and drive into Egypt. Hezekiah's proto-Deuteronomist (and later, even more so, Josiah's Deuteronomist) took the Israelite concept of uniform law and made it Jerusalem's law for Judah and Israel, in theory, for the sake of vastly enlarging the power of a weakened house of David. Hezekiah was free to revise JE on this basis because, in actuality, he had little or no control of territory beyond Jerusalem other than what Assyria allowed him.

Yahweh reappears in Hezekiah's texts. The motif of seeing, frequent in J, reappears. The reference to Yahweh's blessing and the blessing of nations through Abram's descendants are fashioned after J. That Abram's sons will possess the enemies' gate concisely captures one meaning of E. The episode of Joshua's battle against Amalek borrows the divine rod from J, Amalek from J and the Deuteronomistic tradition, and Joshua from the Deuteronomistic tradition.[11] (Why this battle should be written into JE is not clear.)

The proto-Deuteronomistic laws are more discursive than those in E. The concern for a similar justice is spelled out, but there are significant differences from E. In this legal addendum, child sacrifice is required. Menhirs are prohibited. It is doubtful child sacrifice was

10. It remains possible that some parts of Exodus 32–34 and Numbers derive from the court of Hezekiah. These are not dealt with here because they go beyond the bounds of E.
11. In subsequent additions, much more is made of Moses' rod, by P and apparently others. It is not likely to be an E motif, as it does not relate to E's themes, and its genesis fits the methods of Hezekiah's proto-Deuteronomist. For a nuanced study on Exodus 17 and Moses' rod, see Erich Zenger, *Israel am Sinai: Analysen und Interpretationen zu Exodus 17–34* (Altenburg: CIS, 1982), 56–113. Does Hezekiah's revision direct attention to Moses' rod to compensate for Hezekiah's disposal of Moses' bronze snake (2 Kgs 18:4)?

consistently carried out, even within Hezekiah's restricted domain. But it fits the state of critical peril that Hezekiah threw his kingdom into when he rebelled against Assyria. The last sections of the law recapitulate rules that were apparently already present in J, as though Hezekiah wished to stress the necessity of practicing the cult of Yahweh regularly and only in Jerusalem. The final paragraphs of Hezekiah's additions encourage Hezekiah's followers to take heart in the struggle against Assyria, or later Egypt, in the company of the heroic Ephraimite sheikh Joshua, who subsequently becomes the protagonist of the Deuteronomist's account of the conquest of Palestine.[12]

Hezekiah's JE lay available for further revision during the following centuries. Josiah's propagandists made few, if any, changes in it. For them it served as is as a prologue to their great history of the Jerusalemite temple state, now contained in the books of Deuteronomy through 2 Kings. This history starts out with the definition of jurisdiction found in E but soon departs on its own themes, inherited in part from the traditions of Hezekiah that found incipient expression in the eighth-century additions to JE just discussed.

The transformation of JE into the lengthy text we know as the Tetrateuch awaited the emergence of the priestly imperial province of Judah in the early Persian period. The traditions recorded in the P strand, the last of the three great components of the Tetrateuch, included much that goes back to the temple service of the Jerusalemite priests of the Davidic monarchy. In its present form, however, the P strand reflects the disenfranchisement of the Jerusalemite priesthood under Babylonian rule and exile. That the Tetrateuch is a priestly document in its final form owes to the reestablishment of elements of this priesthood two or three generations later under Cyrus and especially Darius. These priests, whose shrine was the restored dynastic temple of the house of David, ruled in the name of David only. With the demise of the house of David, however, there was no longer any point to opposing it, and the anti-Davidic thrust of E was left folded under in the further development of the Bible.

---

12. Joshua was an Ephraimite *wely*, or local hero and patron; by the eighth century he was dead and venerated at his tomb as the symbolic figurehead of a regional patronage network. Although their exact locations are not certain, the most widely favored site for Joshua's tomb, Timnath-Heres, lies just two and a half miles from the most widely favored site of Jeroboam's birthplace, Zeredah; in any case, the two Ephraimite sites could not have been far apart. I owe to Marvin Chaney the intriguing suggestion that the figure of Joshua may have been literarily broached under Hezekiah precisely because of Joshua's possible connection with Jeroboam I. Joshua plays no apparent role in E. Nonetheless, historically, Jeroboam may well have claimed the support of Joshua's ghost, in addition to Ahiya's living person, thus introducing Joshua into the wider politics of Israel, where he became an increasingly powerful symbol until Josiah had him portrayed in terms of his own reconquest of Israel.

CHAPTER FOURTEEN

Fear, Power, and Faith

To Jeroboam I, Israel's revolution against the house of David began and ended with himself, as the new embodiment of the liberated state. Many fighters and factions contributed to the revolt, thousands matched Jeroboam's courage, and his concept of social change owed as much to the possibilities and limits of Palestinian society as to his own imagination. However, once Jeroboam wrested kingship in Israel, the fate of the revolution lay with him and his household. It was this concept of the revolution that E was written to defend.

This did not change the political nature of the revolution, however. Jeroboam rode to power in a rattletrap movement clapped together out of tenuous social bonds, shaky alliances, and dubious loyalties. E is an anxious text infected with uncertainty and the spirit of deterrence, at odds with the confidence of J. In E, peril threatens at every turn. Fortunately, God designs the peril and its resolution. But for E, this assurance craves repeating and indeed must be rehearsed, restated, and reiterated—scarcely allaying the author's or sponsor's disquiet—until the narrative eventuates in a remedy that monarch and strongmen can control, the revolution's jurisdiction and law, and disorder modulates into order. Then the author need no longer protest his reverence, which was exemplified as obedience all along.

Even E's politics of resentment are muted, despite the infamy of their Davidic foil, and this inveterate means of dispelling political discomfort is inhibited. In E, the apprehensions of the probable commoner Jeroboam show themselves resistant to the capricious comforts of the royal court, circumscribed as an Israelite court at that time had to be. It is difficult to avoid recalling the tradition regarding the vexations that afflicted Jeroboam's predecessor Saul in his chieftain's court, two generations earlier. By a tour de force, E turns Jeroboam's fear inside out and makes it the social norm. Fear turns into the highest value. Perhaps Saul might have induced his scribe to write the same thing, if he had won.

To his credit, Jeroboam subscribed to the axiom that a household's well-being, and even that of a ruler, is a function of social order rather than vice versa. Among his ruling contemporaries, the opposite view presumably predominated: the king's palace sustained the social order. To judge from E, Jeroboam's vision extended beyond such aristocratic confines. Life, including changes in rule, is not capricious: it is contingent on obedience, and God tests obedience. The standards of obedience apply to the social whole—a remarkable confession from the spirit of a man who, while having to trust many parties, could really trust only one, his God. E's final pronouncement is that the revolution must be based elsewhere than in Jeroboam. Israel's polity was not yet impaired enough to abet the lawless arrogance of a Solomon or Ahab. The premise of Jeroboam's revolution was calling death what Solomon called life, and Jeroboam was not about to replace Solomon's tyranny with his own.

Social order is a sacred good not to be despised or belittled. However, it remains elusive. What Plato and Aristotle; Hobbes, Locke, and Montesquieu; and Hamilton, Madison, and Jefferson sought to define in the midst of social dislocation in their times, and many others in more recent times, Jeroboam earlier sought to implement. J provided Jeroboam's scribe with a history of power, to which it was quite appropriate to add a history of fear and social order, as both hinged on power. E denies the ruler absolute power. This denial is the *state's* bugbear. All other degrees of power are a matter for human judgment (upon which we can only join Jeroboam in troubled reflection and the attempt to order) and a matter for God's judgment (in which we can have faith).

For what, after all, is politics—jurisdiction included—but the social management of fear and its oppressive ramifications? Power, the apparent antidote to fear, is the end of politics. Power and fear can be reordered not by politics but only by the word of God ("Fear not—I am with you") in its fullest, not partial, application. Religious cult—law included—is the symbolization, or adornment, of politics. Theology is the rationalization of cult symbols; of this E displays little. Faith is the idealization of cult symbols—law included. At the intersection of the fear of God and God's quieting of the fear of common power, E reaches its climax. Fear contributes to faith where the fear of God advances a more just political option.

The E Texts
(Hebrew Versification)

Genesis 20:1–17
21:6, 8–32
22:1–13
28:11aβ, 12, 15, 16aα, 17a, 18, 20, 21a, 22
30:1–3, 6, 8, 17a, 18aα, 18b, 20aα, 22–23
31:3b, 5–16, 19b, 20aβ,° 24, 29, 30b, 32–35, 37–41aα, 41b–42, 45, 50b, 51bα,° 52aβ, 52bβ,° 53b
32:2–3
33:5aβb, 11aβ,° 19–20
35:1–5, 7–8, 14aα, 14b, 17b, 20

37:5–11, 18a, 19–22, 24, 28aα, 29–30, 34aα, 36
39:1bα, 9bβ
40:1–23
41:1–33, 38–39, 50–52
42:1–4, 9a, 18b, 19aβ, 21–24, 28b, 29a,° 33bα, 34bα, 35–37
43:23aα,° 23b, 29b
44:16bα
45:2–3, 5b–8, 9aβ, 15–16, 25–27
46:1b–6aα
47:7–11a
48:1–2a, 15–16, 21b–22
50:15–26

Exodus 1:15–22
2:1–10
3:1a,° 1bβ, 4b, 6b, 9–15
4:17–18, 20b
9:28aβ,° 30 (except "Yahweh")
13:17–19
14:19a
18:1aα,° 1aβ, 2aα,° 5aα,° 5bβ,° 6aβ,° 9aα,° 10aα,° 12–26
19:3a, 16aβb, 17, 19
20:18–21
21:1–37
22:1–16
24:11bα, 13aα, 13b

° = Less than a quarter of the verse; a phrase only.

The "Proto-Deuteronomistic" Texts
within the Scope of E

Genesis 20:18
  21:33
  22:14–19
  28:21b
  30:18aβ

Exodus 9:30 ("Yahweh")
  17:8–16
  22:17–30
  23:1–33
  24:13aβ, 14

For Further Reading

The following are recommended for those who wish to begin to read further in English on the subjects of this book. Readers are reminded that the present book often represents a different point of view, especially on issues dealt with in chapter 1 under the heading "Different Foundations."

Chapman, A. T. *An Introduction to the Pentateuch.* Cambridge: Cambridge University Press, 1911.

Coote, Robert B., and Mary P. Coote. *Power, Politics, and the Making of the Bible: An Introduction.* Minneapolis: Fortress, 1990.

Coote, Robert B., and David Robert Ord. *The Bible's First History.* Philadelphia: Fortress, 1989.

Craghan, John F. "The Elohist in Recent Literature." *Biblical Theology Bulletiin* 7 (1977): 23–35.

Fretheim, Terence E. "Elohist." In *Interpreter's Dictionary of the Bible.* Supp. vol., edited by Keith Crim, 259–63. Nashville: Abingdon, 1976.

Friedman, Richard Elliott. *Who Wrote the Bible?* 70–88. New York: Summit Books, 1987.

Gottwald, Norman K. *The Hebrew Bible: A Socio-Literary Introduction,* 137–38, 152–53, 183–84, 348–51. Philadelphia: Fortress, 1985.

Hauer, Chris, Jr. "The Economics of National Security in Solomonic Israel." *Journal for the Study of the Old Testament* 18 (1980): 63–73.

Jenks, Alan W. *The Elohist and North Israelite Traditions.* Missoula, Mont.: Scholars Press, 1977.

Knight, Douglas A. "The Pentateuch." In *The Hebrew Bible and Its Modern Interpreters,* edited by D. A. Knight and G. M. Tucker, 263–96. Philadelphia: Fortress, 1985.

McEvenue, Sean E. "The Elohist at Work." *Zeitschrift für die alttesta-
    mentliche Wissenschaft* 96 (1984): 315–32.
Wilson, Robert R. "Israel's Judicial System in the Preexilic Period."
    The Jewish Quarterly Review 74 (1983): 229–48.
Winnett, Frederick V. "Re-examining the Foundations." *Journal of
    Biblical Literature* 84 (1965): 1–19.
Wolff, Hans Walter. "The Elohistic Fragments of the Pentateuch." In
    The Vitality of Old Testament Traditions, edited by Walter Bruegge-
    mann and Hans Walter Wolff, 67–82. Atlanta: John Knox, 1975.

Author Index

Subject Index